Aragon

An Introduction to Shared Inquiry

An Introduction

FOURTH EDITION

to Shared Inquiry

A HANDBOOK FOR

JUNIOR GREAT BOOKS®

LEADERS

Wellington Middle School

THE GREAT BOOKS FOUNDATION
A nonprofit educational organization

TEXT AND COVER DESIGN   William Seabright,
William Seabright & Associates

First Printing
9 8 7 6 5 4 3 2 1 0
Printed in the United States of America

Published and distributed by

The Great Books Foundation
A nonprofit educational organization
35 East Wacker Drive, Suite 2300
Chicago, IL 60601-2298

www.greatbooks.org

Contents

Introduction

ABOUT THE BASIC LEADER TRAINING COURSE

Welcome to the Basic Leader Training Course and to Junior Great Books. For more than 35 years, the Great Books Foundation has provided teachers and parent volunteers with outstanding Shared Inquiry leader training through the basic course. The National Staff Development Council has recognized this course for its effectiveness in helping teachers increase student achievement (Joellen Killion, *What Works in the Middle: Results-Based Staff Development,* 1999). School districts nationwide have approved the course for in-service and teacher recertification credit. (Please contact your local school administrator for information.)

Learning how to lead Shared Inquiry is a rewarding experience that requires active and intense participation. Each activity in the course is based on work that precedes it. For these reasons, participants who arrive after the course has begun or who miss any other part of it will not be able to participate further.

In this course, you will learn the interpretive reading strategies for preparing and presenting to students the high-quality, challenging literature contained in the Junior Great Books anthologies. You will also practice our time-proven tech-niques of discussion management, which include following the four rules of Shared Inquiry Discussion, asking effective follow-up questions, and using a seating chart.

ABOUT THIS HANDBOOK

This handbook is to be used in conjunction with the Basic Leader Training Course developed by the Great Books Foundation. During the course, you will have the opportunity to learn about and participate in the method of interpretive reading and discussion known as Shared Inquiry. A unique element of this process is Shared Inquiry Discussion, in which participants, with the aid of a leader, work together to help each other better understand a challenging work of literature. Becoming an accomplished interpretive reader and comfortably adapting to your new role of leader requires time and practice. This handbook is designed to reinforce the training you receive in the course and to serve as a resource as you begin leading Shared Inquiry on your own.

As you begin using Junior Great Books, we urge you to turn to this handbook often. Not only can it help you review what you learned about preparing for and leading discussion, but it also contains useful information on adapting Junior Great Books to meet the needs of your students and the demands of your particular situation. **Questions from the Field** address frequently asked questions. **Classroom Management Tips** speak to issues of concern to the typical classroom teacher. If you are a teacher who plans to use the Junior Great Books Read-Aloud Program with kindergartners and first graders, you will probably have questions about adapting Shared Inquiry for this special audience. The **Read-Aloud Notes** provide advice and explanations that specifically address your needs. **Chapter Highlights** offer an in-depth look at selected topics of interest to all program users. Finally, the **chapter reviews** provide a quick recap of the main points in each chapter.

ABOUT THE GREAT BOOKS FOUNDATION

The Great Books Foundation is an independent, nonprofit educational organization whose mission is to help people learn how to think and share ideas. Toward this end, the Foundation publishes collections of classic and modern literature as part of a continuum of reading and discussion programs for children and adults.

Established in 1947 by a group of prominent citizens led by University of Chicago Chancellor Robert Maynard Hutchins, the Great Books Foundation began as a grassroots movement to promote continuing liberal education for the general public. In 1962, the Foundation extended its mission to children with the introduction of Junior Great Books. Since its inception, the Foundation has helped thousands of people throughout the United States and in foreign countries begin their own discussion groups in schools, libraries, and community centers.

Today, Foundation instructors train more than 12,000 people each year to lead Junior Great Books. The Great Books Foundation derives its income from the sale of books, training fees, contributions, and educational grants.

SHARED INQUIRY

To help fulfill the Foundation's mission, all Great Books programs employ a method of interpretive reading and discussion known as Shared Inquiry. In this distinctive approach to learning, participants search for answers to interpretive questions raised by a text—questions for which the text suggests more than one answer. This search is inherently active, requiring participants to interact thoughtfully with a selection to resolve these questions of meaning. Participants of all ages are encouraged to read the selection (or have it read to them) at least twice, to note their reactions to the text, and to ask questions about its meaning.

Central to this process is Shared Inquiry Discussion. The success of Shared Inquiry Discussion depends on the special relationship between the leader and the group. Instead of imparting information or presenting personal opinions, leaders guide participants to reach their own interpretations by posing thought-provoking questions and following up purposefully on what participants say. In doing so, leaders help participants of every age develop both the flexibility of mind to consider problems of meaning from many angles and the discipline to analyze ideas.

During this course, you will learn how to lead Shared Inquiry Discussion. You will also learn to guide students to give full consideration to the ideas of others, weigh the merits of opposing arguments, and modify their initial opinions as the evidence in a text demands. Your participants will gain experience in communicating complex ideas and supporting, testing, and expanding their own thoughts. In this way, Shared Inquiry promotes thoughtful dialogue and open debate, preparing participants to become able, responsible citizens, as well as enthusiastic, lifelong readers.

A NOTE ABOUT GREAT BOOKS PROGRAMS FOR ADULTS

In addition to Junior Great Books, the Great Books Foundation supports adult book groups through publications, workshops, and other services. Whether you are part of a book group or reading on your own, our reading selections invite you into a great conversation about ideas. The selections are carefully chosen for their rich ideas and quality of writing and are accompanied by thoughtful, provocative questions. The Great Books Foundation offers two reading series for adults:

- The 50th Anniversary Series, in nine thematic anthologies, includes works by both classic and modern authors from around the world.

- The Great Books Reading and Discussion Program anthologies feature provocative selections from classic authors.

Our Junior Great Books program for high school—Introduction to Great Books, which includes shorter selections from the classics as well as some modern fiction—is also often used by adult book groups.

The Great Books Foundation also publishes collections of readings on contemporary issues in conjunction with other educational organizations:

- *A Gathering of Equals,* funded in part by a grant from the National Endowment for the Humanities, is an anthology of texts that examine American pluralism and identity.

■ *. . . And Justice for All* is a joint publication from the Great Books Foundation and the Foreign Policy Association marking the fiftieth anniversary of the United Nations' Universal Declaration of Human Rights.

Discussion group members enjoy both intellectual collaboration and the opportunity to reflect on their own lives and convictions in light of ideas from major thinkers. Many teachers and parents find that participating in a Great Books program not only provides intellectually stimulating discussion but also helps them become better listeners and questioners and is therefore an excellent way to support their leadership of a Junior Great Books program.

Participants in Great Books groups typically meet once a month for a one- or two-hour discussion. The setting is informal, such as a participant's home, a public library, or a church or school. Group members read, take notes, and prepare for discussion independently. Great Books groups may have permanent leaders or several leader-participants who take turns leading discussion. Although training is not required for the establishment of an adult Great Books discussion group, people often find it beneficial to attend either the Basic Leader Training Course or the Adult Program Participant Training, which is specially designed for leaders and participants in adult groups.

Chapter 1

BECOMING FAMILIAR WITH

JUNIOR GREAT BOOKS

The ability to read interpretively not only allows students to engage with and appreciate challenging literature, but also compels them to use and develop several cognitive processes: drawing inferences, weighing evidence, drawing conclusions, making comparisons, and constructing meaning. Interpretive reading is a complex habit of mind, one that needs cultivation over a period of years. For this reason, the Foundation has developed Junior Great Books for kindergarten through high school.

Junior Great Books combines rich, challenging literature with Shared Inquiry Discussion and a full complement of reading and writing activities. The activities support students as they engage in the process of interpretive reading and reflective thinking. When used with the high-quality literature in the student anthologies, the activities help students become more accomplished readers. Students develop their ability to ask relevant questions, trace ideas throughout a story, pause and reflect while they read, look closely at meaningful words and passages, build interpretations, and elaborate on their ideas through writing. By providing students with a way to approach challenging literature successfully, Junior Great Books cultivates a disposition to pursue ideas in depth and develops the skills needed to do so effectively.

This chapter presents an overview of the three programs in the Junior Great Books continuum of learning. Junior Great Books is designed with age-appropriate activities based on the interpretive issues of the Junior Great Books selections, which are chosen for age appeal, literary merit, and interpretive depth. The activities guide students through the process of active reading, note taking, and interpretive thinking and provide opportunities for students to express their ideas orally and in writing.

THE JUNIOR GREAT BOOKS CONTINUUM OF LEARNING

In Junior Great Books, students' natural curiosity fuels the learning process.

Junior Great Books is based on the idea that all students put forth their best intellectual efforts when they are presented with genuine problems of meaning. Students demonstrate surprising acuity and delight in responding to intellectual challenge, and their natural curiosity fuels the learning process. The three programs in the Junior Great Books continuum—the Junior Great Books Read-Aloud Program, Junior Great Books, and Introduction to Great Books—provide an ongoing and coordinated approach, from kindergarten through high school, for developing students' reading, thinking, writing, speaking, and listening skills. The programs enable students with diverse cultural and personal perspectives, learning styles, and levels of ability to contribute and learn from one another. They allow students to build steadily on their own ideas and ensure that each member of the class feels challenged and encouraged to reach his or her highest level of achievement.

The strong oral component—the frequent opportunities for reading aloud and sharing notes, questions, and opinions—invites less-fluent readers to participate on an equal footing with more advanced readers.

JUNIOR GREAT BOOKS READ-ALOUD PROGRAM (GRADES K-1)

The Junior Great Books Read-Aloud Program is designed to help children in kindergarten and first grade experience the pleasures of reading and thinking about meaningful works of literature. The program fulfills basic reading-readiness objectives and aids students in developing critical and imaginative thinking, comprehension, and speaking and listening skills.

In the Read-Aloud program, children focus on one unit (a story or group of poems) over a period of four to five days. Children listen as their teacher, and later a parent or adult partner, reads the story or poems to them. Because children hear the selection read aloud at least three times, all students—both nonreaders and independent readers—can enjoy and comprehend rich literature.

Students develop and express their interpretive thinking about the selection by participating in a variety of activities. In Sharing Questions Discussion, a version of Shared Inquiry Discussion adapted for young participants, children learn from experience how to actively respond to a story or poem by asking and answering questions they find important. Other activities include art projects, dramatizations, and group creative writing. The Read-Aloud student books contain not just the selections but also the art and writing activities for each unit. Completing these activities in their own books allows students to create a unique intellectual product that becomes a tangible source of pride and satisfaction for the beginning reader.

JUNIOR GREAT BOOKS (GRADES 2-9)

Junior Great Books for grades 2–9 develops students' reading, speaking, critical-thinking, and writing skills by means of intensive work with outstanding literature from cultures around the world. By using Junior Great Books in conjunction with independent reading and some direct instruction in grammar, spelling, and phonics, schools can provide an innovative language arts curriculum that develops reading, speaking, listening, and writing skills and is coordinated throughout the elementary and middle school years.

The number of each series corresponds to its recommended grade level, and the interpretive activities in each unit are designed to be appropriate for students at that grade. You may want to use an earlier series to accommodate less-fluent readers, but it is not necessary to adopt a higher series for proficient readers—the selections will present sufficient challenge for the best readers at each level. Similarly, you may find that students needing extra support in the interpretive reading process benefit from participating in interpretive activities modeled after those suggested for students in earlier grades. For that reason, a complete description of all of the activities in the Junior Great Books continuum is given later in this chapter.

Junior Great Books Series 2 serves as a transition between the Read-Aloud program and Series 3–6. As in the Read-Aloud program, students using Series 2 follow the basic activity sequence of two readings in class and one at home, in which they discuss the open-ended questions printed in the margins of their books. Dramatizations and interpretive drawing activities are still offered, but increasing emphasis is placed on interpretive discussion and individual writing. Students using Series 2 also begin to participate in Shared Inquiry Discussion.

Beginning with Junior Great Books Series 3, students are introduced more directly to the strategies of drawing on prior knowledge when reading, using note taking to improve understanding, and looking at the multiple connotations of words through the Text Opener, Directed Notes, and Interpreting Words activities. These activities are facilitated by pages found in the students' interpretive activity books. In addition, a preface that first appears in the Series 5 student anthologies introduces students to Shared Inquiry and explicitly addresses topics such as active reading, taking notes, listening and responding to fellow participants, observing the rules of Shared Inquiry Discussion, and writing interpretive questions.

Junior Great Books Series 7–9 recognize that students in grades 7–9 are ready to exercise more independence in the interpretive reading process. The activities for Series 7–9 follow the Series 3–6 sequence, but are less directive and allow students more autonomy as they engage in interpretive work. Although students in grades 7–9 do not need the structure provided by the activity books, they are still given many opportunities to share thoughts and express ideas during the activities. In Series 7–9, writing is stressed as an integral part of students' ongoing, personal interaction with the text.

INTRODUCTION TO GREAT BOOKS
(HIGH SCHOOL)

Introduction to Great Books engages students in reading some of the finest classic and modern authors and in thinking reflectively about the questions of enduring significance they raise. The timelessness and universality of the selections and the openness of Shared Inquiry make Introduction to Great Books appropriate for a variety of students, including college freshmen and sophomores. Rather than focusing on discrete skills, students in Introduction to Great Books learn to integrate reading, thinking, writing, listening, and speaking skills to achieve the goals of constructing meaning from a challenging text and communicating one's ideas effectively.

Introduction to Great Books is a flexible program in which the full complement of interpretive activities for each selection can be conducted in four or five class sessions, or in as few as two—if the prereading and postdiscussion writing activities and the reading and note taking are done as homework. If so, the first classroom session focuses on the sharing of questions, notes, and preliminary ideas, and the second session is devoted to Shared Inquiry Discussion.

THE JUNIOR GREAT BOOKS MODEL OF ACTIVE READING

> Students not only grasp the facts of a selection but also reflect on the interpretive issues that make the reading so rewarding.

Learning to read interpretively means students in Junior Great Books learn to be active readers. They acquire the habits of noting their reactions to a selection, questioning as they read, noticing important details, and weighing evidence. During Shared Inquiry Discussion, they learn to compare their ideas and insights to those of other readers. The reading and discussion sequence for each Junior Great Books series is designed to help students at each grade level grasp the necessary facts in the selection while they reflect on the interpretive issues the selection raises. The introductions, multiple readings, time to raise questions, note taking, and thoughtful consideration of significant vocabulary guide students through the initial work of establishing the facts while also considering the story's interpretive issues. Hearing the insights of others, comparing ideas, and weighing evidence, as practiced in Shared Inquiry Discussion, aids students in checking their comprehension, analyzing sections of text, judging the reasonableness of opinions, and determining the relevance of inferences. The postdiscussion writing assignments give students an opportunity to extend their thinking about the selection. Through these activities, students move beyond identifying individual words to making sense of the text as a whole—to comprehension in its fullest sense. Engagement in the entire sequence of activities ensures that students work meaningfully with language in all its forms—by reading, listening, speaking, and writing.

INTRODUCING THE SELECTION

At every grade level, teachers are provided with introductory activities to help orient students to the selections they are about to read. Because students in the primary grades have limited experience and knowledge, introductions for younger students supply contextual information. As students progress through Junior Great Books, they are asked to draw on prior knowledge and become more active in the process of interpretive reading.

Grades K–2. In the Read-Aloud program and Junior Great Books Series 2, brief *introductions* provide necessary definitions or references. For example, an introduction may focus on words that students are not likely to know but that are central to understanding the story as a whole. In other cases, introductions may give the setting or location of the story. Because the selections are from diverse cultures, students often need to be made aware that certain unusual words are actually the names of characters.

Grades 3–6. In Junior Great Books Series 3–6, students' thoughtful encounter with a work of literature begins with an activity called a *Text Opener*. Text Openers often give students scenarios that allow them to connect their own personal experience to interpretive issues they will encounter in the story. The Text Opener activity primes students' interest in the story and prepares them to meet potential obstacles to understanding, such as an abstract theme or metaphorical language.

Grades 7–12. In Junior Great Books Series 7–9 and Introduction to Great Books, *prereading questions* prepare students to consider the text in a thoughtful way and to overcome potential obstacles to understanding, such as historical allusions or metaphorical language. Prereading questions may draw on students' prior knowledge of a topic or guide them to do some simple research.

First Reading of the Selection

Because the selections are rich in ideas and vocabulary, all students at all grade levels are asked to read the selections, or hear them read, more than once. Students need to become well acquainted with the facts of the story so they can support their ideas as they work on the interpretive issues. We suggest that the first reading be done orally while students listen or follow along in their books. Hearing the selection read aloud helps students get an overall sense of the story and begin to establish the facts on which they will build their interpretations. It also helps students understand the selection's tone and grasp unfamiliar vocabulary in context.

Reflecting on the Selection Between Readings

In Junior Great Books, students are encouraged to raise their own questions about a work. Immediately after the first reading of the selection is a good time for students to voice initial reactions and raise questions about the selection.

Grades 2–12. In Junior Great Books Series 2–9 and Introduction to Great Books, the teacher takes time to collect students' questions in the *Sharing Questions* activity. Sharing Questions allows students to clear up misreadings, get help with vocabulary, and set the selection more firmly in their minds. More important, forming questions based on their own responses gives students a starting point for interpretive thinking when they read the selection a second time and take notes.

Grades K–I. Although kindergarten and first-grade students often do not understand the story well enough to voice questions after hearing it read aloud only once, in the Read-Aloud program we do recommend that they be given time for *sharing first responses*. This brief, informal exchange after the first reading allows students time to clear up misunderstandings and factual errors. This sharing not only encourages an atmosphere of cooperation but also demonstrates to students that different opinions and reactions are an important part of thinking about literature and are the seeds of original ideas that are worth ongoing reflection. The *art activity* after the first reading is also an important opportunity for reflection on the story.

To give students a better opportunity to turn their reactions into questions, students are prompted to ask a question, labeled *"My Question,"* as part of their at-home work on a story or poem. A sample letter in the appendix of the Teacher's Edition and the "Note to the At-Home Reader" in the front of each volume of the student anthologies give instructions about this part of the activity.

Displaying students' "My Questions" on a bulletin board emphasizes the idea that each child's curiosity about a selection is worth considering and pursuing. Posting these questions fosters the ideal of Shared Inquiry by communicating respect for each child's contribution to the group effort to understand works

Read~Aloud Note

ART AND DRAMA ACTIVITIES

In the Read-Aloud program and in Junior Great Books Series 2, interpretive drawing and dramatizations play an important role in fostering students' imaginative and interpretive thinking about a story. Creating artwork based on a reading selection is an appealing way for children to connect with literature. Dramatizing scenes from a story helps students connect with unfamiliar situations, empathize with characters, form ideas about how different characters interact with one another, and express their ideas.

Art assignments in the Read-Aloud program are specifically tailored to each selection and represent several different types of activities. All art activities and dramatizations conclude with students sharing and comparing their ideas, which allows students to hear perspectives different from their own and move forward in their thinking about the story.

of literature. Additional art and dramatization activities provide further time for reflection and setting the story firmly in mind before students participate in Sharing Questions Discussion, the adaptation of Shared Inquiry Discussion for the Read-Aloud program.

SECOND READING AND NOTE TAKING

During the second reading, students attend more carefully to the details of the selection when asked to do a note-taking activity. Note taking in conjunction with a second reading is practiced throughout Junior Great Books in different forms, appropriate to grade level.

> Do you agree with Timmy Willie that Johnny Town-mouse has been kind? (Circle your answer.)
>
> YES   NO
>
> Why or why not?

Grades K–2. In the Read-Aloud program and Junior Great Books Series 2, students begin to develop the habit of noting their reactions to a text by answering questions provided in the margin. Children in the Read-Aloud program hear the story read the second time at home, where they discuss *G.B.'s questions*—open-ended questions printed in the margin of their books and signaled by the Read-Aloud mascot, G.B. (pictured here).

These at-home questions encourage children to pause and respond to significant moments in the story and prepare students to share their beginning ideas in class. In Series 2, this routine of answering questions that appear in the margin continues, but without the use of G.B. as a mascot.

Grades 3–9. In Junior Great Books Series 3–9, during the second reading of the selection, students are asked to respond to a consistent pattern in the story through the use of a *Directed Notes* prompt provided in the Teacher's Edition or Leader's Guide. Students either put symbols in the margin of the text or underline sentences in response to a specific directive. By providing a focus, the Directed Notes prompt guides students through a challenging text and encourages them to read more carefully and with greater sensitivity to the significance of details. Consistent use of Directed Notes helps students internalize different note-taking strategies and learn how to take thoughtful notes on their own. With experience, students can move to writing words or phrases in their books that express their reactions more fully.

Grades 10–12. In Introduction to Great Books, high school students read and discuss both fiction and nonfiction. The Leader's Guide suggests an interpretive note source, which provides a central, specific issue on which students can focus. In some cases, two note sources are given; either or both of them may be used. Students are also coached in different note-taking strategies for fiction and nonfiction selections.

RAISING INTERPRETIVE ISSUES THROUGH VOCABULARY

Throughout Junior Great Books, students learn to work with and appreciate rich vocabulary.

Grades K–1. In the Read-Aloud program, students are encouraged to work with rich vocabulary by copying words they like from the selection onto the *My Favorite Words* page, found at the end of each volume of the student anthology.

Read-Aloud Note

MULTIPLE READINGS

Because students in the early grades are typically not strong independent readers, three readings are recommended in the Read-Aloud program and Junior Great Books Series 2. Three readings are generally necessary to help students remember the facts and sequence of events in a story or poem. Young students also need help reflecting on the story or poem, and three readings provide more opportunities for this reflection. In addition, since students are familiar with the story by the third reading, they can follow along in their books and, in this way, improve their sight vocabularies.

Grades 2–9. In *Interpreting Words* activities in Junior Great Books Series 2–9, students concentrate on the interpretive dimensions of important words. Through Interpreting Words, students learn how specific words can contribute to understanding the broader interpretive issues of a story and how an author's word choice can provide nuance and depth to characterization.

SHARED INQUIRY DISCUSSION

Shared Inquiry Discussion, in which the leader turns to participants with questions he or she has genuine doubt about, is the best model of the inquiry and collaboration that is at the heart of Junior Great Books.

Grades 2–12. In each Shared Inquiry Discussion, students gain experience in reading for meaning, communicating complex ideas, and supporting, testing, and expanding their own thoughts. Shared Inquiry Discussion helps participants develop the habit of reflective thinking. In *How We Think*, educator John Dewey wrote that reflective thinking is disciplined and purposeful, "the kind of thinking that consists in turning a subject over in the mind and giving it serious and consecutive consideration." It is a process that starts with a problem and moves toward a solution by sifting, relating, and ordering a flow of ideas. By thinking reflectively about an interpretive problem in discussion, participants learn to give full consideration to the ideas of others, weigh the merits of opposing arguments, and modify their initial opinions if the evidence demands it.

Grades K–1. *Sharing Questions Discussion* is similar to Shared Inquiry Discussion, but adapted for younger participants in the Read-Aloud program. It is shorter and based on a group of five or six interpretive questions—some of which the students have contributed themselves. The role of leader remains the same. By asking questions, the leader provides students with an example of a person intellectually engaged by literature.

WRITING

Writing gives students the opportunity to reflect on their own ideas about a selection and then revise, elaborate, and further develop those ideas. In Junior Great Books, students can use writing to develop their ideas in a variety of ways—supporting opinions with evidence, relating events in the story to their own lives, using events in the story in creative writing, or evaluating the story in light of their own experience and values.

Grades K–1. Group creative writing assignments, which occur in most Read-Aloud units, appear late in the suggested sequence of activities and are intended to give students an opportunity to consolidate some of their previous interpretive work and to think further about some aspect of the selection. Kindergartners and first graders learn that writing is a process as they contribute ideas or rhyming words and make other suggestions for the group writing projects.

Grades 2–6. In Junior Great Books Series 2–6, interpretive activity pages prompt students to reflect on a selection as the week progresses. The emphasis in most of this work is not the production of highly polished essays but the use of writing as a means of assisting thinking about a story's characters and themes. Postdiscussion writing prompts and graphic organizers on the activity pages support students as they plan their stories, poems, evaluative essays, or personal essays.

Grades 7–12. In Junior Great Books Series 7–9 and Introduction to Great Books, students are prompted to use writing throughout the interpretive reading process to reflect upon and develop their ideas. Students' thoughtful engagement with an interpretive issue begins with writing a brief answer to a prereading question and continues as they note their reactions to the text on both first and second readings. After discussion, students can use their previous written work on the unit to help them address in depth an interpretive or evaluative question of interest to them.

Grades 2–12. Used in conjunction with Shared Inquiry Discussion, the Building Your Answer activity page helps students further develop their opinions in writing. Students examine their answers to a basic interpretive question and see what points need to be made or what evidence needs to be supplied. Completing this page at the end of discussion allows students to see how ideas they heard changed their interpretations.

THE SUGGESTED SEQUENCE OF ACTIVITIES

A unit of Junior Great Books includes two readings of the selection, interpretive reading and writing activities, and Shared Inquiry Discussion.

The process of interpretive reading and discussion remains fundamentally the same for all students, but the activities that guide them through the process take into account developmental differences. As you think about integrating Junior Great Books into your classroom schedule, you should refer to the following suggested sequence of activities for the series you will be using. The sequence for each series provides a model of full use of the program: students participate in Junior Great Books daily, making use of all of the interpretive activities and completing one unit per week, on average. (Please note that some series also include novellas. These longer works are not intended to be completed in one week.) If your classroom schedule does not allow for daily use of the program, you may want to consider conducting the activities over a two-week period.

JUNIOR GREAT BOOKS READ-ALOUD PROGRAM

SUGGESTED SEQUENCE (GRADES K-1)*

SESSION 1

Introduction and first reading of the selection

Sharing first responses

Interpretive art activity

AT-HOME WORK

Reading of the selection by parent or other
    adult partner

Answering of G.B.'s questions

Child's dictation of "My Question" to parent or
    adult partner

SESSION 2

Posting students' "My Questions"

Third reading of the selection

Discussion of children's answers to G.B.'s questions

Creative activity (dramatization or art)

SESSION 3

Sharing Questions Discussion

Textual analysis (may include dramatization)

SESSION 4

Additional creative activity (dramatization or art)

Evaluative discussion

Group or individual writing of poems, songs,
    or paragraphs

*This sequence may vary in specific units.

JUNIOR GREAT BOOKS SERIES 2

SUGGESTED SEQUENCE (GRADE 2)

SESSION 1	Introduction and first reading of the selection
	Sharing of first responses/questions
	Writing down a question student has about the story
AT-HOME WORK	Second reading of the selection
	Sharing of responses to at-home questions with parent or other adult partner
SESSION 2	Third reading of the selection
	Sharing responses to at-home questions
	Writing an answer to an interpretive question
SESSION 3	Interpreting Words, textual analysis, or dramatization
SESSION 4	Shared Inquiry Discussion
	Optional activity: choosing a question from the Junior Great Books bulletin board and writing a response
SESSION 5	Creative writing, personal essay, or evaluative writing
	Dramatization

JUNIOR GREAT BOOKS SERIES 3–6

SUGGESTED SEQUENCE (GRADES 3–6)

SESSION 1	Text Opener (introduction of the story)
	First reading of the story
	Sharing Questions
SESSION 2	Second reading with Directed Notes
SESSION 3	Interpreting Words
SESSION 4	Shared Inquiry Discussion
SESSION 5	Creative writing, personal essay, or evaluative essay

JUNIOR GREAT BOOKS SERIES 7–9

SUGGESTED SEQUENCE (GRADES 7–9)

SESSION 1   Answering a prereading question

First reading of the selection

Homework: completing first reading and writing down
   initial questions about the selection

SESSION 2   Sharing Questions

Second reading with Directed Notes

Homework: completing second reading and taking notes;
   writing interpretive questions (optional)

SESSION 3   Sharing notes and interpretive questions

Interpreting Words

Homework: preparing a passage for textual
   analysis (optional)

SESSION 4   Shared Inquiry Discussion (including textual analysis)

Homework: completing the Building Your Answer
   activity page

SESSION 5   Postdiscussion writing

Homework: revising and finishing writing

INTRODUCTION TO GREAT BOOKS

SUGGESTED SEQUENCE (HIGH SCHOOL)

SESSION 1

Answering a prereading question

First reading of the selection (first interpretive note source on nonfiction selection)

Homework: completing first reading and writing down initial questions about the selection

---

SESSION 2

Sharing students' questions about the selection

Second reading with interpretive note source (second interpretive note source on nonfiction selection)

Homework: completing second reading and taking notes; writing interpretive questions (optional)

SESSION 3

Sharing notes and interpretive questions

Homework: preparing a passage for textual analysis (optional)

SESSION 4

Shared Inquiry Discussion (including textual analysis)

Homework: completing the Building Your Answer activity page (optional)

SESSION 5

Postdiscussion writing

Homework: revising and finishing writing

THE JUNIOR GREAT BOOKS LEARNING OBJECTIVES

Students develop many skills while reading for meaning.

Becoming a self-reliant thinker, reader, and learner results not from mastering a skill, or even a set of skills, but from having confidence in one's ability to deduce answers to complex questions. This confidence is achieved through repeated successful experiences in which children read for understanding and communicate their ideas effectively—using many different skills at once.

We believe that all children have the capacity to improve the skills, adopt the attitudes, and cultivate the intellectual habits necessary to consider problems from different perspectives and to analyze ideas. The interpretive reading process practiced in Shared Inquiry, and given structure in Junior Great Books, is one of the best ways for students to have these successful experiences. Students use their skills not in isolation but in combination in order to discover answers to questions that are important to them and to express their ideas clearly both in speaking and in writing. However, most state and local educational objectives list skills separately. Therefore, to aid you in aligning Junior Great Books with your local educational standards, we have identified specific skills students develop by using the Shared Inquiry approach to learning.

READING

- *Reading Comprehension*
Reading for comprehension involves various reading skills and strategies. Ultimately, comprehension requires moving beyond recognizing the meanings of individual words to fully understanding the ideas behind the words. Throughout Junior Great Books, the focus of reading is on understanding the ideas presented in the selection. Students analyze the author's tone and purpose through the exploration of interpretive questions. When giving evidence to support their answers, students recall details and cite specific passages relevant to the topic under discussion.

- *Reading Strategies*
Students in Junior Great Books practice both silent and oral reading. They learn to devote at least two readings to a challenging work of literature and to employ different strategies on each reading. Students take notes during the first reading to gain a sense of the story as a whole. Students are also encouraged to use their own questions about a selection as a tool for further exploration. Note taking during the second reading helps students find patterns or connections in the text.

- *Vocabulary*
Students learn to use strategies for working with challenging vocabulary, ones that also increase their comprehension of the selection. Students derive the meanings of words through context, explore the multiple dimensions of highly significant words, and examine the images suggested by metaphorical language.

THINKING

Junior Great Books is widely recognized as helping students develop higher-order thinking skills. The program's focus on reading and interpreting challenging literature gives students ample practice in identifying problems of meaning presented by a text. Students learn to resolve these problems of meaning by considering others' opinions, weighing evidence, drawing inferences from the text, and using sound reasoning to form and revise their opinions.

WRITING

Students in Junior Great Books use writing activities to clarify thinking, synthesize information, and acquire understanding. Students take notes; write questions as a means of responding to issues presented in a text; and write stories, poems, evaluative essays, or personal essays to extend their thinking about the issues raised during discussion.

SPEAKING

With Junior Great Books, students have many opportunities for oral work. From reading the stories aloud to participating in Shared Inquiry Discussion, much of the work in a unit can be done orally. Both the leader's follow-up questioning and the interaction between participants prompts students to offer evidence from the story to support their opinions, to state their ideas clearly, to explain their reasons for an inference or conclusion, to defend positions, and to agree and disagree with others in an appropriate manner.

LISTENING

In Shared Inquiry Discussion, the leader models listening by paying close attention to participants' comments, noting their ideas on a seating chart, and posing questions in direct response to what participants say. The leader also encourages active listening and a cooperative attitude by asking questions that encourage participants to respond to each other's statements, assist one another in recalling the facts of the selection, and explain their ideas. In turn, students begin to listen for different ideas, ask each other for clarification, raise objections to unsupported propositions, and incorporate the ideas of others into their interpretation of a text.

Chapter Highlight

Criteria for Choosing the Junior Great Books Selections

Our criteria for deciding which selections to include in our series are determined by our primary educational goal: to develop in all students the skills, habits, and attitudes that characterize successful readers, ones who think for themselves and have the persistence of mind to reach for meaning. To accomplish this end, Junior Great Books uses the Shared Inquiry method of interpretive reading and discussion. Shared Inquiry focuses on interpretive questions—fundamental questions about the meaning of a work that invite many answers, based on the text. This unique emphasis on interpretation shapes the following four criteria.

1. *Selections must support extended interpretive discussion.* Because students in Junior Great Books participate in a collaborative search for meaning in a work, selections must invite and support a number of interpretations. Selections that are rich in ideas, and in which the author's meaning is not explicit, raise the interpretive questions necessary for sustained Shared Inquiry Discussion. And only well-crafted selections, works that are thematically complex and cohesive, suggest real answers—that is, interpretations that can be supported with evidence from the text rather than merely being a matter of personal opinion.

2. *Selections must raise genuine questions for adults as well as students.* Providing selections that speak to both leaders and students helps ensure that Shared Inquiry Discussion will be a collaborative effort. Leaders must experience the same kind of curiosity about the text that they want to encourage in their students. Leaders, in sharing what they find puzzling or thought-provoking, express their own intensive engagement with the work. By providing a model of an inquisitive reader, leaders guide students through the complex and rewarding intellectual process that characterizes Shared Inquiry.

3. *Selections must be limited in length.* A manageable length allows students to read each selection at least twice and work with it closely. Through concentrated work on a single text over a period of several days, students in Junior Great Books learn how

to read closely—to examine details and draw connections—always with the purpose of working out answers to substantial questions of interpretation. Short stories and novellas are well suited to this intensive work.

4. *Selections must be age appropriate.* When deciding which series to place a selection in, we give primary consideration to the appropriateness of a selection's theme and style for a particular grade, rather than to standard assessments of reading levels. At all levels of Junior Great Books, students encounter the original words of the author: no texts have been modified to meet a controlled vocabulary.

Read-Aloud Note

SELECTION CRITERIA

The stories and poems in the Read-Aloud program are of the same high quality as all Junior Great Books selections. To ensure that selections can support the sustained attention they receive in the program and hold children's interest for an extended period of time, all have passed through a stringent and lengthy review process.

1. Read-Aloud selections are emotionally compelling and imaginatively engaging. For children to develop a love of reading, they must be exposed to literature that speaks to their feelings and experience. Stories that strike a profound chord in children help them learn that reading is more than a basic processing of information; it is an inexhaustible source of pleasure and insight.

2. The Read-Aloud selections are well written. Vivid language and strong, evocative images convey the delights of the written word. Children soon discover that words contain meaning and associations that can be explored, played with, and savored.

3. Read-Aloud selections embody interpretive ideas and themes meaningful to both children and adults. When words are rich in meaning, children feel their efforts to read and understand them are rewarded. As children work with the stories and poems, they develop confidence in their own perceptions and become motivated to learn to read for themselves. Moreover, selections that have as much meaning for adults as for children help ensure that Shared Inquiry will be a collaborative effort among teachers, parents, and children.

Like all the Junior Great Books anthologies, the Read-Aloud volumes feature literature from a variety of cultures, including African, Arabian, Caribbean, European, Hindu, and Native American. Each selection embodies universal themes that all children can readily embrace—themes such as fairness, friendship, growing up, and learning about people and nature. By pursuing these themes with classmates in an environment of Shared Inquiry, children gain experience in exploring their own unique perspectives and enlarging their understanding of ideas common to the human experience.

Chapter Review

1. Interpretive reading is not a single skill but a complex habit of mind that must be developed over time.

2. Junior Great Books combines rich, challenging literature with a method of interpretive reading and discussion known as Shared Inquiry.

3. Shared Inquiry is an active reading process in which students note their reactions, question as they read, notice important details, weigh evidence, and test their ideas against those of their classmates as they work toward full comprehension of a text.

4. The sequence of developmentally appropriate interpretive activities that accompanies each selection supports students in the process of interpretive reading and discussion, helping them become self-reliant thinkers, readers, and learners.

5. When integrated into your language arts curriculum, Junior Great Books provides the basis for an ongoing, coordinated approach to developing students' reading, listening, speaking, writing, and critical-thinking skills, which are at the heart of the interpretive reading process.

Chapter 2

READING INTERPRETIVELY

To guide your students to find meaning in a text, you must become an interpretive reader yourself. Being an interpretive reader involves reading actively, raising questions, and striving for understanding. An interpretive reader wants to know why the characters in a story act as they do and what the unusual or surprising events in a story mean—in other words, what an author is trying to communicate.

This chapter will take you through the process of interpretive reading—the process that your students will learn with your guidance. Since Shared Inquiry is a process of raising questions and turning to others for help in finding answers, the first step in leading is to discover what you yourself do not understand about the selection. In finding the questions that most interest you, you will become more familiar with the work as a whole. This familiarity with the text, in turn, will enable you to respond more effectively to ideas that your students offer—and to discover what in the selection is prompting those ideas. Your Teacher's Edition or Leader's Guide will support you in this process as you work with your students.

READING ACTIVELY AND TAKING NOTES

Reading actively means reading twice to boost comprehension and find new problems of meaning.

Because Junior Great Books selections are unusually rich in ideas, it is necessary to read them at least twice. By reading the selection carefully twice and noting your reactions to the work, you will come to terms with the ideas of the selection in your own way. Noting your responses will also help you develop confidence in your understanding of the selection and allow you to identify those particular problems that hold your interest.

On your first reading, concentrate on getting a sense of the work as a whole. When reading fiction, for example, think about what happened in the story and why. Ask yourself: Why did the author want to tell this story? How do the characters and events make sense in light of my own experience? When reading nonfiction, try putting the author's argument into your own words. Give yourself some time between readings to let your ideas and impressions settle.

Your second reading will let you refine and correct first impressions, answer many of your initial questions, and find some new problems of meaning. You may want to concentrate on specific portions of the selection that interest or puzzle you, analyzing them and relating them to the work as a whole. Because you already know the outcome of the story or understand the general thrust of the author's argument, you can more clearly recognize the connections among incidents in the plot or points in the argument. Having the author's "big picture" in mind as you read will also make unusual word choices and recurrent ideas and images more noticeable. Note any word that the author seems to use in a special way and trace it throughout the work to understand what it means in different contexts.

Some leaders find it helpful to distinguish the notes from their first and second readings. They use different-colored pens or different markings, or switch from pen to pencil. Leaders also find it helpful to do the note-taking activity for the unit, suggested in the Teacher's Edition or Leader's Guide, on their second reading. Here are some general note-taking suggestions:

- *Note anything you don't understand.* If a character says or does something that puzzles you, note it in the margin. If you find some aspect of an author's argument unclear, make a note of what perplexes you.

- *Note anything you think is especially important.* Look for those passages that strike you as particularly significant. Try to express exactly why they attract your attention and hold your interest. If you have a question about an essential part of an author's argument, write it in the margin. Note also the connections you perceive between different parts of the selection. If you begin to see a pattern in the author's use of language or in a character's actions, make a note to remind yourself to look again at related passages.

- *Note anything you feel strongly about.* If you disagree with an author's argument, make a note about why you differ. If a character's actions trouble you, explain your response in the margin. Noting your agreement can be equally useful.

Looking for such genuine problems of meaning in the selection—those that persist as problems even after careful reflection—is one of the aims of this reading and note-taking process. But often at this stage, you cannot be sure if something is truly problematic or if it can be easily resolved with a little more thought. For this reason, you should be open-minded and jot down any reactions you have. Be alert to all the possibilities of meaning you see in the selection, and don't be overly concerned with assessing your responses.

By morning they grew right up to the sky.

Pages from "Jack and the Beanstalk,"
Junior Great Books Series 2,
First Semester

Teacher's Edition with
leader's notes

JACK AND THE BEANSTALK

English folktale
as told by Joseph Jacobs

There was once upon a time a <u>poor</u> <u>widow</u> who had an <u>only son named Jack</u> and a cow named Milky-white. And all they had to live on was the milk the cow gave every morning, which they carried to the market and sold. But one morning Milky-white <u>gave no milk and they</u> <u>didn't know what to do.</u>

why?

desperate situation

"What shall we do, what shall we do?" said the widow, wringing her hands.

"Cheer up, mother, I'll go and get work somewhere," said Jack.

Naive? Optimistic?

①

141

① The leader's notes: Orange notes are from the first reading and black from the second. Making notes helps the leader identify what in the text is prompting ideas and what some of those ideas may be.

Textual Analysis Questions

Why does the old man ask Jack such an odd question before offering to swap the beans for Jack's cow?

Why does the man say he doesn't mind doing a swap because Jack is so sharp?

Does Jack believe what the man tells him about the beans?

*Would **you** trade Milky-white for the strange-looking beans? Why do you think Jack does?*

❧

Why does Jack think he's getting a good bargain?

Why does Jack think it would be a good thing to have beans that grow right up to the sky overnight?

•••

why not? "We've tried that before, <u>and nobody would take you</u>," said his mother. "We must sell Milky-white and with the money start a shop or something."

"All right, mother," says Jack. "It's market day today, and I'll soon sell Milky-white, and then we'll see what we can do."

So he took the cow's halter in his hand, and off he started. He hadn't gone far when he met a funny-looking old man who said to him: "Good morning, Jack."

"Good morning to you," said Jack, *cautious?* and <u>wondered how he knew his name.</u>

"Well, Jack, and where are you off to?" said the man.

"I'm going to market to sell our cow here."

Even scattered marginal comments help the leader begin to identify the interpretive issues in the selection. One note from the first reading poses a question about something not understood: "What makes him decide [to trade the cow for the beans]?" (page 143). Other notes express emotional responses ("cruel" on page 145), offer judgments about characters' words and actions ("Odd!" and "flattery"), or indicate observations about things that seem important ("Man never said" the beans are magical, on page 144, and "She [the mother] plants beans," on page 145).

···

"Oh, you look the <u>proper sort of chap</u> to sell cows," said the man. "I wonder if you know how many beans make five."

flattery

"Two in each hand <u>and one in your mouth</u>," says Jack, as <u>sharp as a needle.</u>

Is this silly or clever?

Odd!

"Right you are," says the man. "And here they are, the very beans themselves," he went on, pulling out of his pocket a number of strange-looking beans. "As you are so sharp," says he, "I don't mind doing a swap with you—your cow for these beans."

Sarcasm? or <u>praise</u>?

"Go along," says Jack. "Wouldn't you like it?"

Helping or taking advantage?

"Ah! you don't know what these beans are," said the man. "If you plant them overnight, by morning they grow right up to the sky."

"Really?" says Jack. "You don't say so."

"Yes, that is so, and if it doesn't turn out to be true you <u>can have your cow back.</u>"

Guarantee!?

"Right," says Jack, and hands him over Milky-white's halter and pockets the beans.

What makes him decide? Smart or foolish?

Would you trade Milky-white for the strange-looking beans? Why do you think Jack does?

②

143

On the second reading, new responses are noted: Is Jack's answer "silly or clever?" and "Guarantee!?" Earlier notes are reconsidered and some guesses are made about their meaning: Was it "smart or foolish" of Jack to trade the cow for five beans? Some overlooked details now seem important: Is "sharp as a needle" meant as "sarcasm or praise"?

② In the students' books for the Read-Aloud program and Junior Great Books Series 2, questions in the margins prompt students who are not yet able to take notes to reflect on the text and consider their reactions to it.

···

Back goes Jack home, and as he hadn't gone very far it wasn't dusk by the time he got to his door.

"Back already, Jack?" said his mother. "I see you haven't got Milky-white, so you've sold her. How much did you get for her?"

"You'll never guess, mother," says Jack.

"No, you don't say so. Good boy! Five pounds, ten, fifteen, no, it can't be twenty."

"I told you you couldn't guess. What do you say to these beans; they're <u>magical</u>, plant them overnight and—"

③

man never
said this

③ The lines printed beside the text in the Teacher's Edition indicate that this passage would be a good one for close reading, or textual analysis, by students.

Textual Analysis Questions

"What!" says Jack's mother. "Have you been such a fool, such a dolt, such an idiot, as to give away my Milky-white, the best milker in the parish, and prime beef to boot, for a set of paltry beans? Take that! Take that! Take that! And as for your precious beans, <u>here they go out of the window</u>. And now off with you to bed. Not a sip shall you drink, and not a bit shall you swallow this very night."

So Jack went upstairs to his little room in the attic, and sad and sorry he was, to be sure, as much for his mother's sake as for the loss of his supper.

At last he dropped off to sleep.

When he woke up, the room looked so funny. The sun was shining into part of it, and yet all the rest was quite dark and shady. So Jack jumped up and dressed himself and went to the window. And what do you think he saw? Why, the beans his mother had thrown out of the window into the garden had sprung up into a big beanstalk which went up

cruel

<u>She</u> plants beans

Why isn't Jack worried about disobeying his mother?

Why does Jack's mother now call Milky-white the best milker in the parish?

Why is Jack as sad and sorry for his mother's sake as for the loss of his supper?

④

145

④ The suggested textual analysis questions in the margin of the Teacher's Edition page
  may be helpful in leading this passage in a close reading. (See Textual Analysis, pp. 87–89.)

DISTINGUISHING INTERPRETIVE QUESTIONS FROM FACTUAL AND EVALUATIVE QUESTIONS

Interpretation begins with the questions that come to us as we read.

After carefully reading a complex story or essay twice and taking notes, you will probably have many questions about why things happen the way they do or what the author is trying to communicate. In Shared Inquiry, we distinguish three kinds of questions you might ask about a work: factual, interpretive, and evaluative.

In fiction, any information the author provides about the world of the story—every detail of setting, character, and plot—is a "fact," whether or not it corresponds to our perception of reality. For example, in "Jack and the Beanstalk," it is a fact that ogres live in the sky. In nonfiction, the author's statements—propositions, lines of argument, conclusions—are facts.

An appreciation of the facts of a work lays the foundation for interpretation, although complete mastery of the facts is not necessary to begin the process of interpretation. Interpretation begins with the questions that we ask ourselves as we read. Why does a character act in a certain way? Why does the author include a particular detail? Why do things turn out as they do? What does a certain word mean in context? As we develop answers to such questions, we get a better sense of how the parts of the work fit together and what the work means.

When we evaluate a work, we consider its bearing on our lives and its broader implications, even if it poses ideas that seem inconsistent with our own values and personal experience. We judge what the author has written, deciding for ourselves whether it is true.

A thoughtful interpretation can only be achieved by carefully considering the facts the author presents. Similarly, a solid understanding of the author's meaning provides the basis for intelligent evaluation.

FACTUAL QUESTIONS

A factual question has only one correct answer that can be supported with evidence from the text. It asks participants to recall something the author says, and can usually be answered by pointing to a passage in the selection. For example, the answer to the question *What does Jack take from the ogre the first time he goes up the beanstalk?* is explicitly stated in the text: a bag of gold.

Sometimes, however, a factual question cannot be answered by pointing to any single place in the text. Instead, its answer must be inferred from other facts available in the selection. For instance, the answer to the question *Does Jack plan to steal from the ogre when he climbs the beanstalk for the first time?* does not appear explicitly in the story. But we can conclude that since this was Jack's first climb (a fact), he could not have known about the ogre and so could not have planned to steal from him (reasonable inference). Since this inference represents the only logical conclusion, we consider it a fact of the story. The question *Does the golden harp want to go with Jack?* is also factual for the same reason: although the answer does not appear explicitly in the text, it can be inferred with reasonable certainty from other evidence that is explicit. The fact that the harp cries out for its master is sufficient proof that it does not want to go with Jack.

INTERPRETIVE QUESTIONS

An interpretive question has more than one answer that can be supported with evidence from the text. It asks participants to look carefully at what happens in a story and to consider what the story means. For example, consider the question *Why does Jack make the third trip to the ogre's house?* Several answers are possible. Jack may have been driven by curiosity or by greed to see what else the ogre had in his house. Perhaps he longed for further adventures or took pleasure in outwitting the ogre. Or, Jack may have wanted to prove himself to his mother or been worried that the hen might stop laying, just as Milky-white had gone dry. The text provides reasonable support for each of these answers. Because the question raises a substantial problem of meaning and can be answered in more than one way, based on evidence in the story, it is capable of sustaining a rewarding discussion.

EVALUATIVE QUESTIONS

An evaluative question asks us to decide whether we agree with the author's ideas or point of view in light of our own knowledge, values, or experience of life. Since an evaluative question asks for a comparison of your views with the author's, the answer depends as much on your interpretation of the text as it does on your knowledge, experience, and values. Consider the question *Is it necessary to take risks—as Jack does—in order to grow up and be responsible?* Participants will be prepared to address the broad issues in this evaluative question only after coming to their own understanding of how Jack behaves and matures throughout the story. If evaluative questions are introduced prematurely, before the meaning of the work has been fully explored, they tend to invite digression and discussion of matters having little to do with the selection itself.

* * *

In Shared Inquiry, we concentrate on interpretive questions, referring to the facts of the work for evidence and reserving evaluation for the time when our interpretation is complete.

DEVELOPING INTERPRETIVE QUESTIONS FROM YOUR NOTES: GOOD SOURCES FOR QUESTIONS

Reviewing your notes is an excellent way to develop interpretive questions. As you look back over the selection, think again about why you noted particular passages, and write down your ideas in the form of questions. Some of the notations you made may no longer seem significant, but others will suggest ideas that continue to hold your interest. At this point, the wording of your questions is not as important as finding genuine problems of meaning that you want to explore further. You can always revise your questions later.* Notes that focus on the following ideas and details are especially good sources for interpretive questions.

> Good interpretive questions that will hold your students' interest come from your authentic engagement with the text.

See Improving Your Questions, pp. 53–57.

CHARACTER MOTIVATION

Look for notes that question the reasons behind a character's statements, actions, or thoughts. For example, you might be curious about why the ogre's wife seems to betray her husband by helping Jack. This might lead you to ask the question *Why does the ogre's wife want to keep Jack from being eaten? Is she impressed with Jack's bravery? His politeness? Or is she moved by how hungry and desperate Jack sounds?*

STRIKING OR UNUSUAL USE OF LANGUAGE

You might be surprised at the way an author expresses an idea or casts a description. For example, thinking about Jack's reply to the funny-looking old man might lead you to ask this question: *Why does Jack answer the old man's question by saying, "Two in each hand and one in your mouth"?* Does Jack's answer indicate that he is worried about the future, and where his next meal is coming from? Does his answer suggest immaturity—or a quick wit?

PROMINENT DETAILS

Although you will not want to question the purpose of every detail, some details can function as important elements in an interpretation. Consider the question *Why does the author make Jack's mother a poor widow?* Does it seem significant to you that Jack is poor and fatherless? What bearing does this information have on our understanding of Jack's adventures? Expressing your question about how to interpret a detail you noted can lead your group to a fresh understanding of a story or essay.

WORDS OR PHRASES WITH MULTIPLE INTERPRETATIONS

Often, the way a word or phrase is used will attract your attention and cause you to consider whether it has special significance. If examining the context of the word or phrase doesn't help you pinpoint a definite interpretation—and, in the case of a striking word, if a dictionary does not seem to settle the matter—then write a question that calls attention to the ambiguity you find. For example, the author writes that even after his second trip up the beanstalk, Jack was "not content." But why does Jack feel this way? Does he want more gold, or does he long for further adventures? Your curiosity about Jack's feelings could lead to the interpretive question *Why isn't Jack content even though he has riches to last a lifetime?*

CONNECTIONS BETWEEN PASSAGES, CHARACTERS, INCIDENTS, OR IDEAS

The various parts of a well-crafted work of literature are interconnected and support one another. Discovering the meaning of a story or essay depends on understanding the relationships between its parts. In "Jack and the Beanstalk," Jack's three adventures in the sky are similar in many respects—the climb, the theft, the escape—but their parallels also highlight significant differences. If you note that on his second trip Jack confronts the ogre's wife in a more assured manner, you could ask *Why is Jack so much bolder in asking the ogre's wife for food on his second trip than on his first?* Is he just hungry, as he was before? Is he gaining time to look around? Is he braver—or is he being foolhardy? In this case, comparing parallel scenes spotlights Jack's developing confidence and cleverness. Examples of other connecting questions include *Why does the author have the ogre's wife treat Jack more kindly than his own mother does?* and *Why does the author have Jack take a bag of gold, a magic hen, and a golden harp, in that order?*

* * *

The most important source of interpretive questions is your thoughtful consideration of what the entire work seems to mean. After reading a selection the second time, go over passages that seem especially significant or striking, such as those involving a moment of crisis or a decisive change in a character. Then step back and ask yourself what, in broad terms, are the work's major themes and ideas. For instance, thinking about the changes Jack undergoes in the course of his adventures could lead you to ask the question *Why do Jack's adventures enable him to grow up successfully in the story?* Often, considering a more comprehensive problem of meaning will change the focus of other questions and bring new interpretive issues to mind.

CHOOSING A QUESTION TO LEAD IN DISCUSSION: ELEMENTS OF A GOOD INTERPRETIVE QUESTION

Shared Inquiry Discussion should be a process of discovery for both you and your participants. When you ask an interpretive question to start discussion, in effect you are saying, "Here is a place in the text that suggests something important to me, but I'm having trouble deciding what it means. With your help, I would like to think more about this problem." You want your students to be able to respond—and to want to respond—when they hear your initial question. You want them to understand right away what you are asking and to be able to think about what details in the selection bear on the problem you have raised.

To choose a good interpretive question, one that can get your students interested immediately, consider the following five criteria.

DOUBT

You should have genuine doubt about the answer or answers to the question. Doubt means that after identifying and considering a problem of meaning, you are still unsure about how best to resolve it. The problem persists, and so you want to share the question with your group to find out what they think about it.

To be sure that you have doubt about a question, try to write at least two different answers and support each with evidence from the selection. If the text seems to provide reasonable support for at least two answers, and you're not sure which you prefer, then for you that question raises a point about which you have doubt. For example, in "A Game of Catch," it would be difficult to have doubt about the answer to *Is Scho as good a ball player as Glennie and Monk?* because the text plainly indicates that the answer is no. Likewise, *Do Monk and Glennie try to exclude Scho from their game?* is not suitable for Shared Inquiry Discussion because it has only one reasonable answer based on the evidence in the story.

Doubt does not mean, "I know the best answer, but my students may not." Questions meant to lead your participants to a single answer or to an insight that you think is important are not suitable for Shared Inquiry Discussion because such questions do not help participants work with and develop their own ideas. Be aware of how a question, by its wording or assumptions, may imply a predetermined answer. For example, the question *Don't you think the title "A Game of Catch" refers to more than Monk and Glennie's game?* tends to push students to answer yes. Similarly, *Do you really think Scho fell from the tree accidentally?* seems with the word *really* to betray the leader's lack of doubt about the answer.

INTEREST

Your question should be about an interpretive problem that truly interests you. Your enthusiasm for a question can be contagious, leading to a lively exchange of ideas among your students. If you ask a question you don't care about, your participants will sense your lack of interest and respond superficially with whatever they imagine will quickly bring discussion to a close. It is easier to keep discussion moving by following up on what students have to say if the question matters to you.

DISCUSSIBILITY

Your question should be discussible. Does the question send you to the selection for answers? And does the selection contain the evidence needed to support answers? Sometimes, a work captures us so thoroughly we lose track of the limits of the world that the author has created. The question *How will Glennie and Monk react the next time they are playing catch and Scho comes along?* inquires about a period of time not encompassed by the selection, and so involves speculating beyond the facts of the story. Questions that ask what would have happened had events in the work been different are also speculative, for example: *How might the story have turned out if Glennie and Monk hadn't made Scho wait so long?* Finally, some questions about specific details, such as *Do you think maybe Scho can't afford a glove? What grade is Scho in?* or *What do you imagine Scho's home life is like?* are not discussible because answers cannot be supported with evidence from the text. Unlike a good interpretive question, these questions will fail to keep participants grounded in the text and moving toward a fuller understanding of the story.

CLARITY

Your question should be clear. An interpretive question should be easy for your participants to understand; other-wise, they will have to spend valuable discussion time simply trying to figure out what the question means. Consider how your students would respond to the unnecessarily difficult language in this question: *Does Scho exhibit symptoms of delusion in his verbal attempts to control Glennie and Monk?* A question that is poorly focused will also seem unclear: *Why does the author have Scho climb up to what he calls a "wonderful seat," and which the author later calls a "cradle of slight branches"?* Both of these questions would stump most participants. In writing questions, strive for a clarity and sharpness that will prompt your students to begin thinking of answers right away.

SPECIFICITY

Your question should be specific. First, it should be specific to the selection. If a question can be applied to many other selections with only a few word changes, it is probably too general. *How are Monk and Glennie alike and unlike?* and *What is the main idea of the story?* are examples of overly broad questions that could easily be altered for use with other stories. Such questions do not give participants a definite problem to explore, nor will they spark the interest of your students. To bring a problem of meaning into focus and to avoid getting vague responses, make your question as specific to the selection as you can.

Second, your question should specify the place in the selection to which you wish to direct attention. A question such as *What does Scho want?* is not specific because there are several places in the story where it is uncertain what Scho wants. Different answers to this question may be the result of students thinking the question is about different parts of the story rather than a true disagreement in answers. What Scho wants at the beginning of the story may differ from what he wants at the end, but these are two separate problems. A question that fails to distinguish between these two problems can cause needless confusion and make it difficult to keep discussion on track.

Questions from the Field

How can I lead a discussion if I can't think of any questions I have doubt about?

If, after a first reading, you feel you have no doubt about what the author is trying to say, the solution may be as simple as allowing yourself time between your first and second readings of the selection. Interpretation is a reflective process and requires some patience. Giving yourself time between your first and second readings may be all that is necessary to see the story in a new light.

If you find it hard to think of questions because you are not moved by the story, ask yourself what is preventing you from connecting with the story. Do you lack sympathy for the characters? Is the story's setting too unfamiliar? Are you uncomfortable with the story's themes or ideas? Identifying the stumbling block will ease you over it because you can use it to formulate a genuine question for yourself.

For example, you might think after a first reading that "Tiger-Tiger!" from *The Jungle Books* (Series 5, Second Semester) isn't very interesting because it's "just a boy's adventure story." If you get stuck in this way, try to elaborate on your perception: What are some of Mowgli's adventures? Thinking about such passages may lead you to such questions as *Why does the wolf pack try to cast Mowgli out? Why can't Mowgli adjust to village life?* and *Why is Mowgli finally able to defeat Shere Khan?*

Your Teacher's Edition or Leader's Guide is also a source of ideas. Look at the interpretive questions provided, and write down two or more answers for each. By answering these questions, you will become familiar with some of the

story's interpretive possibilities and uncover new areas that you will want to explore in discussion. The Teacher's Editions for Junior Great Books Series 3–6 also provide sample responses to some of the activities. These responses may help you see things from another perspective.

Your students are another source of help. As you guide them through the reading, take some time to let them ask questions about the selection. Another possibility is to ask a colleague to prediscuss the story with you (see Preparing with a Colleague, p. 63). This is a good way to hear and entertain a different perspective on the selection. Or, ask a friend or relative to read the story and talk about your questions with you—you will have fun, and you will find that your companion's viewpoints will help to open up your thinking.

IMPROVING YOUR QUESTIONS

Many of the questions you write after your second reading of the selection will need to be reworked or revised before discussion. Some will turn out to be factual, evaluative, not fully developed, or unclear. Or you may find that several weaker questions can evolve into a single question that better expresses a particular problem. Sometimes you will write several versions of the same question. To decide which formulation of a question is best, you must estimate what will get your participants to react. While there are no rules for transforming your initial questions into interpretive questions that are sharply focused and provocative, the following guidelines will help you revise your questions.

REVISE QUESTIONS WITH ONLY ONE ANSWER

If a question turns out to be factual, or if you eventually come to lack doubt about it, check to see if its answer will lead you to an interpretive question by revising it to include a reasonable assumption.* For example, your initial thinking about "A Game of Catch" might lead you to ask *Does Scho play a game of his own?* The answer to this question—Scho does indeed play his own game in pretending to control Glennie and Monk—suggests the interpretive question *Why does Scho play a game in which he pretends to control Glennie and Monk?* This revision, unlike the original question, has a number of different answers because it explores Scho's motives.

For more about assumptions, see p. 75.

REVISE EVALUATIVE QUESTIONS

If a question on your list is evaluative—*Is Scho wrong to interfere with Glennie and Monk's game?*—reword it so that instead of calling for a judgment it asks about a problem of meaning in the text, such as *Why does Scho interfere with Glennie and Monk's game?* The original question asks participants to judge Scho's behavior, while the revision encourages them to discuss Scho's motivation using evidence from the story. Similarly, *How could Monk and Glennie have been nicer to Scho?* would probably lead to moralizing, rather than to a deeper understanding of the story. A revision such as *Why do Glennie and Monk allow Scho to wait more than five minutes without giving him his turn?* asks students to think about the motives of Glennie and Monk.

CLARIFY WORDING

Clarify the wording of a question to get rid of abstract terms. Words like *good* or *evil* can make your question unclear because, although familiar, they can have definitions that are vague or value laden. The question *Are we to conclude that Scho is evil at heart?* could result in a semantic tug of war between participants who have different ideas of what "evil at heart" means. Difficult vocabulary or jargon can also make your questions unintelligible for some participants. The question *Does Scho play his game for ego gratification?* assumes that your participants have a knowledge of psychological terminology. In both instances, revising the question, either to *Why does Scho pretend he can control Glennie and Monk?* or *Why does Scho continue to taunt Glennie and Monk even after they invite him to come down and play catch?*, addresses the problem of Scho's motivation in more direct terms suggested by the text.

AVOID LITERARY TERMINOLOGY

Questions that use or ask about literary terms suggest that participants need a particular vocabulary to appreciate literature and that discussion is merely a technique for teaching literary terminology. Questions such as *Is Scho a tragic hero? How does the author foreshadow Scho's unhappy end? Is "A Game of Catch" an allegory of the fall of man? Are there any important symbols in the story?* can inhibit a free exchange of ideas by making students feel that they are being tested in discussion. Moreover, it is quite difficult to maintain your own doubt about the answers to such questions. You should revise general questions about what something "represents" or "symbolizes," using the author's own words if possible. Instead of *Is Scho's falling from the tree symbolic?*, ask *Why does the author have Scho play his game in a tree?* or *Why does the author have Scho fall from the apple tree?*

PRESENT ALTERNATIVES

Present distinct alternatives, where possible. Be alert to interpretive problems that require a choice between two plausible answers that are in especially strong opposition. If you have genuine doubt about which of the answers is preferable, then instead of leaving the question open, state the alternatives for your participants to weigh. For example, the question *Why does Glennie ask Scho if he has his glove, when it's obvious that he doesn't?* could be revised this way: *Is Glennie's question "Got your glove?" an invitation for Scho to play or a way of getting rid of him?* Such a question can make discussion more interesting because participants will have to take a stand and choose between competing points of view. Be certain, though, that the alternatives you offer in the question are the ones most strongly suggested by the selection. If several other answers are equally plausible, your question could restrict inquiry.

MAKE VAGUE QUESTIONS SPECIFIC

The question *What is Scho's attitude toward Monk and Glennie?* might not give participants enough information about the problem you want them to consider. Scho's attitude toward the boys, which changes in the course of the story, would be better explored through more specific questions, such as *Why does Scho say he can make Glennie and Monk do whatever he wants?* and *Why doesn't Scho accept Glennie's invitation to come down from the tree and play catch?*

RETHINK QUESTIONS THAT INCLUDE THE AUTHOR

Many interpretive issues can be phrased as either a problem of character motivation or a problem of the author's intention. However, the addition of "the author" to a question like *Why does Scho climb the tree?* will alter the type of answers you hear in discussion. Do you want your participants to talk about Scho's reasons for climbing the tree—or the author's reasons for having him do it? In a case like this, be sure to use the form of the question that reflects the problem you want to explore with your group.

In reviewing such questions, consider whether you should shift the focus from the author to the characters. For example, the question *Why does the author have Scho continue his game after Monk apologizes to him?* will force your group to think about Scho from an unnecessarily distant perspective. Instead, asking *Why does Scho continue his game after Monk apologizes to him?* will get your participants to explore Scho's motives and feelings more directly.

On the other hand, the question *Why are Glennie and Monk so good at their game?* is less suited for Shared Inquiry Discussion than *Why does the author make Glennie and Monk so good at their game?* The first question would elicit only speculative answers—perhaps the boys were naturally athletic or played together often—that would not lead participants to a greater understanding of the story. The second question, however, raises the larger—and more discussible—matter of why Glennie and Monk's skill is important to the story.

✳ ✳ ✳

Improving interpretive questions is not a science. The phrasing you choose represents your best judgment about what will most clearly convey an interpretive problem as you see it and what will most effectively get your participants involved. Consider the following variations on the question *Why does Scho pretend to control Glennie and Monk?*, which appears in the Teacher's Edition for Junior Great Books Series 5, Second Semester:

> *Does Scho pretend he controls Glennie and Monk
> because he wants to disrupt their game or because
> he wants to be included?*
>
> *Why does Scho play a game that disrupts Glennie
> and Monk's game of catch?*
>
> *Does Scho disrupt Glennie and Monk's game out
> of spite or because he wants to be noticed?*

Although each of these questions has a slightly different focus, they all concern Scho's motivation for playing his game—and they all would be suitable for Shared Inquiry Discussion. When improving your interpretive questions, keep in mind that there is no such thing as the "perfect" wording. Refining ideas—including your own—is part of the process of Shared Inquiry. In discussion, you should be flexible about your questions and be ready to rephrase them if your participants need help in responding.

PREPARING BASIC QUESTIONS AND CLUSTERS

You will begin discussion with a basic question that invites many answers.

Although writing and answering your own interpretive questions prior to discussion is excellent preparation for leading, you are not restricted to those questions when conducting Shared Inquiry Discussion. Your Teacher's Edition or Leader's Guide provides a wealth of questions, and your students may offer additional questions that you will want to consider during discussion.

Once you have written or selected several interpretive questions that you are interested in pursuing, you need to think about how you will be using them in discussion. Which questions address major problems and themes? Which probe more specific details? What are the relationships among the questions? Which question should you use to begin discussion? To determine the relative importance of each question, and to put into sharper perspective the larger, more comprehensive problems of meaning suggested by the work, we suggest grouping your questions into clusters.

Grouping interpretive questions involves putting together those questions that bear on the same problem of interpretation and then identifying—or writing—a basic question for each group. A *basic question* is one that comprehensively addresses a central problem of meaning in the selection. Since answering a basic question satisfactorily requires examining many passages in the text, it is a good question with which to begin discussion.

A *cluster* is a basic question plus a group of interpretive questions that are all related to the basic question. The questions in a cluster might approach the problem in the basic question from different perspectives, address separate parts of the problem, or examine various passages that bear on the problem.

A leader working on "A Game of Catch" might develop a cluster that looks something like this:

Basic question: *Is the story suggesting that Glennie and Monk treat Scho unfairly?*

Is Glennie's question "Got your glove?" an invitation for Scho to play or a way of getting rid of him?

Why does Glennie invite Scho down from the tree to play catch?

Why does Monk apologize for causing Scho's fall from the tree?

Why does Monk begin to throw the ball to Glennie once or twice before he gives Scho the hard, bumpy grounder?

The basic question examines Glennie's and Monk's behavior toward Scho. The question addresses a central problem of meaning—why the characters interact as they do. It is comprehensive because it looks at the boys' behavior in its totality yet retains a sharp, clear focus. The question is not vaguely stated or hard to understand. For these reasons, this question is a good one for beginning discussion.

The interpretive questions in the cluster help to answer the basic question because they direct attention to passages containing relevant evidence. Each question refers to a point in the story when Glennie's or Monk's motives are in doubt: Glennie's ambiguous question, "Got your glove?"; his suggestion that Scho climb down from the tree; Monk's apology; and his hard throw to Scho. Asking a number of related questions—rather than an assortment of unrelated ones—will make your group's exploration of the selection more thorough and coherent. But a cluster is only a provisional plan for helping your participants resolve the comprehensive interpretive problem posed by your basic question. Discussion itself will determine which questions from the cluster you will use and when to use them.

Questions from the Field

Do I always have to organize my questions into basics and clusters?

In certain instances you may decide that a basic question and cluster is not the best way to organize your interpretive questions for discussion. Students in the Read-Aloud program, for example, may have a difficult time dealing with a basic question simply because it is comprehensive. They may need the support of sequentially organized questions (see Sharing Questions Discussion, pp. 92–93).

At other times the text may seem to resist easy organization of questions. For poetry or some nonfiction selections, grouping together questions about the same passage may help you understand the author's intent even if it is not clear how the questions are related.

Finally, you may not have doubt about a basic interpretive question for the selection and wish to explore lesser interpretive issues about which you do have doubt. In these cases, prepare 10–12 interpretive questions (with all the qualities of good interpretive questions) and organize them in a way that seems most helpful to you. Although this list should not be a rigid agenda for discussion, the work of organizing the questions will help you see possible links among the questions and determine when to introduce them into discussion.

You can prepare clusters from your interpretive questions by following these steps:

1. *Group your questions.* Place together those that seem to deal with the same problem of meaning. When you are finished, you may have three or four groups, each containing several questions that concern an interpretive problem you wish to explore. To test whether a question belongs in a given cluster, begin to answer it. If answers to the various questions begin to build on each other, they are related. Some questions will not seem to fit with any of the others. Put these aside.

2. *Select or write a basic interpretive question for each cluster.* Examine each group to determine whether it contains a question that states the problem in a comprehensive fashion. If no question in the group seems "basic," ask yourself what all the questions have in common. Then, write an interpretive question to cover the main issue the cluster addresses. If you have trouble writing a basic question, one of the questions for discussion printed in bold in your Teacher's Edition or Leader's Guide may provide the unifying focus your cluster needs.

3. *Develop the clusters.* You should have four or five questions in each cluster. If your cluster falls short, consider whether any of the questions you have set aside can be revised and included, or write additional questions to fill out the cluster as necessary. Check to see whether the answers to each question in the cluster will help you answer the basic question. If two questions bring up similar answers, discard the question that seems less clear. If a question is only a close restatement of the basic question, drop it or revise it. Do the same with your other clusters. If you have trouble grouping your questions into clusters, the sample interpretive questions in your Teacher's Edition or Leader's Guide may provide some help.

After working with your questions and grouping them, you will find that some of your clusters address problems that seem more comprehensive, more essential to the meaning of the work, or more interesting to you. Select one of these clusters for your group to discuss first. It is the basic question from this cluster that you will use to initiate Shared Inquiry Discussion.

It is very possible that your class will spend the entire discussion time on one basic question and its related questions. However, it is a good idea to have a cluster in reserve in the event your participants tire of or thoroughly explore the initial question before time is out.*

See Closing the Discussion, pp. 90–91, and Classroom Management Tip, p. 91.

Chapter Highlight

Preparing with a Colleague

Working with a partner will make your preparation more enjoyable and will also make you a more confident leader. This prediscussion gives you the opportunity to share your thinking about a selection, refine your questions, generate new ones, and develop clusters. It is also the best way to try out your questions to decide which ones you will ask your group.

TEST YOUR QUESTIONS.

When you meet, bring along your Teacher's Edition or Leader's Guide and all the notes and questions you have written. Test your questions on each other, checking to see whether they might be answered in more than one way based on the selection. Keep track of where you find relevant evidence in the text; this will make it easier to direct participants to important passages. If the two of you strongly disagree about how to answer a question, then you've probably hit on an excellent question to ask your group. Also, exploring differences between your interpretations will sometimes help you come up with new and more interesting questions.

REFINE YOUR QUESTIONS.

As you go through your questions, continue to rethink and improve them. Then select your best questions and check them to make sure they are clear, specific, and thought-provoking. Sort the questions into clusters, following the steps suggested on pages 61–62. Finally, choose the cluster that you will use to start discussion.

REVISIT YOUR QUESTIONS.

Distance often improves judgment, so try to let a day or two pass between writing and reviewing your questions. You might also want to compare your questions to those printed in your Teacher's Edition or Leader's Guide. These questions can supplement your thinking, serving as another point of view when you are ready to decide which questions you want to ask in discussion.

Chapter Review

1. To prepare for Shared Inquiry Discussion, read the selection at least twice and take notes to mark interesting passages, indicate insights, ask questions, and comment on the selection's structure.

2. From your notes, identify genuine problems of meaning—those that you still find puzzling after two readings and some reflection, and that you can interpret in more than one way based on the text. To address these problems, write as many interpretive questions as you can.

3. Sort the interpretive questions you have written into groups of questions that seem related to the same problem of meaning. In each group, try to identify one interpretive question that most comprehensively addresses that group's central concern. This type of comprehensive interpretive question is known as a *basic question*. A basic question and its group of related questions is a *cluster*. If you are uncertain about your questions, turn to your Teacher's Edition or Leader's Guide for help, or prepare questions with a colleague.

4. Select one cluster for your group to discuss first. The basic question of this cluster will be the one you use to begin discussion. Have a reserve cluster for use in the event your initial interpretive problem is exhausted before the end of your discussion time.

Chapter 3

LEADING SHARED INQUIRY

DISCUSSION

In Shared Inquiry Discussion, your role as leader is crucial in helping students attain a more comprehensive understanding of the selection. After you and your students have had an opportunity to read the selection twice, take notes, and raise and reflect upon some of the interpretive issues in the selection,* Shared Inquiry Discussion is an opportunity to explore an interpretive problem in depth. Because the leader does not provide answers, participants are challenged to think for themselves. By trying out ideas and exchanging and examining opinions, students build their own answers to interpretive questions and develop their own ways of understanding the selection.

See suggested sequences of activities, pp. 21–25.

Many users of Junior Great Books find that leading Shared Inquiry Discussion is the most challenging—and rewarding—aspect of the program. For this reason, we have devoted an entire chapter to Shared Inquiry Discussion. This chapter will take you through the steps of leading a Shared Inquiry Discussion and advise you on asking the follow-up questions that make a discussion successful.

DISCUSSION GROUP SIZE

A discussion group should be large enough to ensure that a variety of ideas are expressed but small enough so that everyone also has a chance to clarify and support their ideas. A group of between 10–20 students, with an ideal average of 15, is recommended.

If you have more than 20 participants, try to divide the group for Shared Inquiry Discussion (see Dividing Your Class for Discussion, pp. 94–95). If you cannot divide your class, you may want to consider guiding students through their reading and note taking during class time. This arrangement will give everyone a chance to participate and develop their ideas over the course of work on the selection.

CREATING A GOOD ENVIRONMENT FOR DISCUSSION

Before you begin discussion, you should consider the arrangement of the classroom, make sure that students understand the four rules of Shared Inquiry Discussion, and create a seating chart to help you keep track of ideas that arise during discussion.

SETTING UP THE CLASSROOM

First, try to arrange the room so that everyone can see and hear each other. Second, be sure your students have a convenient surface on which to place their books, open them up, and refer to them regularly. Ideally, students should sit around a table, but if this is not possible, choose a space in which they can sit in a circle or square. This type of arrangement, in which all members of the group can listen and talk directly to one another, stimulates discussion and helps students realize that the ideas offered by their fellow participants can be a major source of insight into a selection. It also helps reinforce your role of partner in Shared Inquiry.

OBSERVING THE RULES OF SHARED INQUIRY DISCUSSION

By observing the four rules of Shared Inquiry Discussion, you and your students will make the best possible use of your discussion time. Rule 1 ensures that participants hear and discuss informed opinions about the reading under discussion. Without the common ground of a shared text (rule 2), discussion could quickly become confused because no one would agree about the facts of the story. When everyone has read the same version, they can work together, looking closely at specific story details, in order to explore significant

THE FOUR RULES OF SHARED INQUIRY DISCUSSION

1. Only those who have read the selection may take part in the discussion.

Participants who have not either read the selection or had it read aloud to them cannot support their opinions with evidence from the text or make sound judgments about what others say about the work.

2. Discussion is restricted to the selection that everyone has read.

This rule gives everyone an equal chance to contribute because it limits discussion to a selection that all participants are familiar with and have before them. When the selection is the focus of discussion, everyone can determine whether facts are accurately recalled or opinions are adequately supported. Talking at length about students' personal experiences or values, or their opinions about other books or movies, is not relevant to the interpretation of the text and may exclude other students from discussion.

3. All opinions should be supported with evidence from the selection.

In Shared Inquiry Discussion, participants are asked to give support for their answers. Making sure that students support their ideas with evidence from the text encourages them to think for themselves and promotes careful reading.

4. Leaders may only ask questions, not answer them.

Your job as leader is to help yourself and your participants understand a selection by asking questions that prompt thoughtful inquiry. If students get the impression that you have "the" correct answer, they will look for you to supply it instead of developing their own interpretations.

OBSERVING RULE 1

The best way to make sure students have read the selection prior to discussion is to give students several opportunities to read the selection, or hear it read. You can read the story aloud to students, as we recommend, or you can assign class time for reading, form partnerships with parents or others to read to students, or establish a "listening corner" with the Junior Great Books audiotapes.

If these efforts fail—for example, if a student was absent when this work was done—ask the student who has not done the reading to sit back from the group and read the selection. Once the student has completed the reading, he or she may rejoin the group. This reinforces rule 1 of Shared Inquiry Discussion for both the student who has not read the selection and those who have.

problems of meaning. For this reason, rules 2 and 3 together reinforce participants' comprehension and recall of the selection while setting the standard for how opinions are weighed. Rules 3 and 4 emphasize students' responsibility for expressing and supporting their own ideas. By exercising this responsibility, students learn to value their own thinking and to respect the opinions of others.

In Junior Great Books Series 2–4, the rules of Shared Inquiry Discussion are printed in the appendix of the Teacher's Editions, in a format suitable for photocopying. You can read the rules to students or make copies for them to keep. In Junior Great Books Series 5–9 and Introduction to Great Books, the rules are printed in the preface of the student anthologies. Having the rules printed in their own books allows students not only to read the rules but to read and understand the reasoning behind them.

In the Read-Aloud program, students are best introduced to the rules by your leading them through the interpretive activities and by a brief explanation. Tell students that the questions they will be discussing are interpretive—they have more than one possible answer—and that you will be asking them to give their reasons (evidence) for their answers. Explain that this will help everyone better understand the answers given.

USING A SEATING CHART

Once everyone is seated, make up a seating chart and write your question at the top of the chart. During discussion, use your seating chart regularly to note ideas and comments next to students' names. Jotting down the comments that you want to pursue immediately, as well as those you decide to table until later, keeps good ideas from getting lost and lets you give recognition to the participants who initiated them. By keeping track of who said what, you can ask, for example, "Kathy, why do you disagree with what Devin said before, that Jack is a thief?" Or, "So, Tiara, are you agreeing with Bill that Jack climbs up the beanstalk again because he's bored?" When participants hear names attached to ideas and opinions, they begin to listen to each other and use each other's thinking to build interpretations.

Here is what a seating chart might look like in the middle of a discussion of the basic question *Why does Jack climb the beanstalk the third time?*

Basic question: Why does Jack climb the beanstalk the third time?

The following tips will help you use your seating chart more effectively as well as improve the quality of your group's discussion.

Keep your notations short. All you usually need is a word or phrase to indicate important ideas. For the first few discussions, you may want to simply make check marks beside the names of students who contribute during discussion.

Develop your own shorthand. Having a set of symbols that you use every week will make note taking more automatic and allow you to write more information in less time. Use initials for the characters' and authors' names. Simple arrows or broken lines can indicate agreement or disagreement between participants. If a student has tried repeatedly to contribute to the discussion, or has said something that you chose to table for some time, put a star by her name so you remember to return to her later. Put question marks by the names of participants who offer comments that you do not understand initially and want to pursue further.

Slow down. Ideas should not get away from a leader. If you find it difficult to keep up with the pace of discussion, then it is probably going too fast for any contributions to be thoughtfully considered by the rest of the group. Do not hesitate to ask, "Would you wait a moment while I write down that idea?" Or ask a student to repeat or rephrase his idea so you can note it on your chart. With older students, you may even want to have them keep their own notes to get everyone involved in tracking the group's responses.

* * *

While using a seating chart will take some practice, over time your notes will prove to be an invaluable aid in sustaining discussion. By slowing down and consistently referring to your chart, you can recall and pursue ideas that would otherwise get lost in the rush of other contributions. You will also provide a strong impetus for students to consider ideas other than their own by showing that you, as a leader, care enough to write down what they say. Displaying your filled-out chart when discussion is over will help make your group aware of how their comments contributed to a fuller understanding of the selection. And finally, your follow-up questions—created from the notes you make throughout discussion—will help you and your class explore individual answers more fully and move everyone toward a more satisfying interpretation of the selection.

Questions from the Field

Why shouldn't I praise my students for giving good answers? I've been told that I must give them feedback on all activities.

As a discussion leader, you will want to encourage participation by showing your genuine regard for students' ideas without endorsing their comments as the "right" way to think. You can do this in several ways:

- Looking at your students when they make their comments lets them know that you are listening intently to what they are saying.
- Writing down students' comments on your seating chart and showing the class your notes after discussion shows that you wanted to remember the ideas students offered.
- Using follow-up questions that encourage students to expand on their initial thoughts indicates your strong interest in helping them deepen their understanding of the story.
- Giving students plenty of time to answer your questions, or even repeating a question, allows them to think carefully and make comments that accurately reflect their thoughts and opinions about the story.

Responding in these ways will help students know that you recognize their abilities to think about and understand significant interpretive issues in literature. After a discussion, you may want to take a few minutes to point out instances in which the group worked well together on a difficult interpretive problem and to compliment all the participants for their efforts. Such praise of the group lets students see progression in their own interpretive skills, reinforces positive attitudes regarding capabilities, and generates great enthusiasm for discussion.

BEGINNING THE DISCUSSION

Letting students think about your question on their own develops independent thinking.

Shared Inquiry Discussion begins when you ask your group a basic interpretive question that will serve as the focus. To help maintain this focus, it is best for participants to have the question before them during the entire discussion. Have students write the question on a blank sheet of paper or on the Building Your Answer activity page. (You can make copies of this page from the master provided in your Teacher's Edition or Leader's Guide, or you can order sets for the classroom.) Having participants write down the basic question makes them pay close attention to its specific wording.

Give students a few minutes to reflect on the question and compose their answers before you ask them to share their ideas. Directing them to record their preliminary answers provides students an opportunity to think more deeply about their answers and prepares them to listen more actively to one another. You may want to suggest that students either mark the text or write page numbers of the places in the selection that help them think about the question you have posed. In this way, even students who are unsure about an answer can still contribute productively to the discussion and will not have to resort to "I don't know" as their only response.

This procedure can be modified depending upon the age of your participants and their reading and writing abilities.

See Sharing Questions Discussion: A Variant for Read-Aloud Participants, pp. 92–93.

If your group is composed of younger children, instead of having them write the question, you may want to put the questions you are going to ask on the board or on chart paper. If your group includes students reading below grade level, you might want to distribute copies of your question beforehand. In short, use your judgment to eliminate needless frustrations that might distract your participants from their main task—communicating their ideas about the selection in response to your basic question.

After a few minutes or when everyone seems ready, repeat the question and ask one participant by name to give his or her answer. Be sure to emphasize that these early answers are merely the beginning of discussion and participants shouldn't feel they must remain committed to their initial ideas. On the contrary, having a record of their first thoughts lets students see how opinions often undergo revision when people share their thinking.

CONDUCTING THE DISCUSSION

To lead Shared Inquiry Discussion successfully, you need to be involved with the ideas and opinions your participants express. Throughout discussion, you must assess each comment, follow up on comments with questions that further discussion, and keep the group moving toward answering your basic question.

GUIDELINES FOR DISCUSSION

The following guidelines will help you maintain your role as leader, encourage participation and interaction, and ensure the thoughtful examination of evidence. These elements are necessary if students are to compare ideas and insights with their classmates to arrive at sound, well-supported interpretations of the selection.

Ask follow-up questions often. Your consistent questioning keeps students attentive to the central problem and helps them refine their answers. You want to help students share, test, and clarify their thinking and, ultimately, resolve for themselves the problem of meaning you have posed. You do this by asking follow-up questions. A few of your follow-up questions will come from the clusters of interpretive questions you wrote during your preparation,* but most will be your spontaneous

See Preparing Basic Questions and Clusters, pp. 58–62.

responses to your participants' comments. This follow-up will allow you to clarify ideas, elicit evidence in support of opinions, pursue intriguing lines of thought, and invite new responses to your initial question.*

For specific suggestions, see Asking Effective Follow-up Questions, pp. 77–83.

Turn to the text frequently. Make a habit of getting students to locate and read aloud passages that support what they say. Ask, "Ben, where is that line in the story about Jack not being content?" Or, "Miyako, what in the story makes you think that Jack likes adventure?" Going back frequently to the text helps students pick up details that they may have forgotten or that they missed during their own reading. It also gives everyone a chance to check opinions offered in discussion against the evidence in the selection.*

One way to make turning to the text more productive is to conduct textual analysis of a passage. See Textual Analysis, pp. 87–89.

Be persistent in striving for answers to your basic question. Stay with a basic question until you believe the group has fully explored it. Ask questions that help students relate their current thinking to the basic question: "Sulema, can you explain how your idea that Jack is greedy helps us answer the opening question?" Keep everyone on track by occasionally repeating the basic question. You can easily do this by asking students to read their answers from the Building Your Answer activity page. If you leave a basic question, be willing to return to it if someone indicates that there is more to say.

Be patient. Participants need time to consider the ideas that come up in discussion. If you call for new opinions before ideas have been fully clarified or explored, many of your participants will offer inadequate or irrelevant answers or will not respond at all. There are several ways you can keep discussion from moving too fast. Pause for a few seconds after asking a question; when students answer, help them clarify their responses before you move on. If someone missed a comment, ask the student who offered the idea to repeat it. Check frequently to see if others understand what is being said. Take the time to frame a follow-up question carefully or to rephrase one that does not seem to be clear to your participants. Let the group hear you think out loud. Taking notes and referring to the comments on your seating chart will also slow the pace of discussion.

Encourage students to speak directly to each other. In Shared Inquiry Discussion, participants broaden their individual interpretations of a text by exchanging ideas about its meaning. Encourage this exchange by getting students to ask each other questions and to answer each other directly, rather than use you as a go-between. Say, "Jessica, could you tell Jason why you disagree with his point that . . . ?" Or, "Devin, would you explain to Kathy why you think differently?" In this way, you reinforce students' responsibility for the content and success of Shared Inquiry Discussion, and you emphasize your own role as a fellow inquirer.

Be open to challenges to any assumptions in your questions. You are free to incorporate reasonable assumptions into your interpretive questions, but your participants are also free to object to them. Your assumption may involve an idea that some students do not agree with or may not yet see for themselves. If a participant seems uncomfortable with a question, ask why. Consider a challenge to your question a useful opportunity: sorting out the reasons for disagreement will help clarify the problem to be discussed.

Give everyone a chance to contribute. Try to call on each student several times. Marking your seating chart when someone speaks will help you keep track of participation. Put a check mark by a student's name each time he or she speaks. Then you can call on students who talk less often to get them involved. Do not let a few articulate students dominate discussion—make it a point to address questions to those who

Questions from the Field

What should I do about students who will not speak during discussion?

Creating an environment in which students feel comfortable sharing ideas may take some time. Some students are naturally more open and talkative than others. Students who are reticent may need some practice speaking in front of others.

Even though you may know your class well, consider taking names for your seating chart at the beginning of each discussion by having each student say his or her name. Giving each student the opportunity to say his or her name ensures that their first contribution will be successful and nonthreatening. Another possibility is to let each student make a short comment about the story to begin discussion.

Students who are usually outspoken during other classroom activities may be quiet during Junior Great Books because they are used to finding the "right" answer. They may be unfamiliar with the open-ended nature of the questions asked during Shared Inquiry Discussion and, as a result, may lack confidence in their ability to answer "correctly." Allowing these students to answer factual questions that come up in discussion, or to read passages of the text if they are good readers, may give them the security they need to begin to answer interpretive questions. Often, students will begin to volunteer more in-depth answers after they have had a few successful experiences in discussion.

Students sometimes remain silent because they need more time to collect their thoughts. Having students fill out the Building Your Answer activity page allows them time to compose their thoughts. Asking a student to read from the activity page is also a good way to involve a shy participant. If a student will not read from the page, collect these pages at the end of the

discussion. Write encouraging comments on the reluctant participant's paper and ask that student to share his or her ideas next time.

Students may also remain silent if they are confused by the leader's question. If you suspect this may be the case, try rephrasing your question or directing the group's attention to the passage that led you to ask the question in the first place.

Finally, the leader's attitude in asking questions can also help to establish the tone of the discussion. The use of follow-up questions demonstrates a degree of acceptance of unusual responses and makes it clear that all contributions to discussion are welcome and worthy.

Gradually, students learn that it is acceptable to have different opinions and that even if their opinion is not supported by the majority, it is still a valid opinion as long as it is supported by evidence from the text.

speak rarely or not at all. In time, shy students can become eager participants if you make a gentle but persistent effort to draw them out.*

See also Shared Inquiry Discussion: A Troubleshooting Guide, pp. 117–121.

ASKING EFFECTIVE FOLLOW-UP QUESTIONS

To think of follow-up questions, listen carefully to what each participant is saying during discussion. Try not to be so concerned about asking your cluster questions that you miss what is being said. Think each comment through: Is the participant's idea clear? Is it relevant? Does it need to be supported with evidence from the selection? Are others in the group likely to understand it? Does it have implications for answering your basic question?

If you're feeling stuck, remember to ask why and where questions— Why do you think so? Where in the story do you see that?

Preface each of your questions with the student's name to give him or her time to focus on your question and to direct the group's attention to that person. If you address questions to the group as a whole, those who like to talk will always respond first and others might not participate at all. Or several people may start talking at the same time.

When you follow up on students' comments, don't paraphrase or summarize what they have said—having words put in their mouths can make students feel that you will be doing their thinking for them. Pay close attention to their wording. The exact phrasing they use might suggest subtle differences of opinion or new ways to relate one comment to another. Listening intently also communicates to your students that their thoughts are valuable.

In some cases your natural reaction will be to ask one of your prepared cluster questions. Other situations will prompt you to other uses of follow-up questions, described below. (All examples of dialogue are from Shared Inquiry Discussions of "Jack and the Beanstalk," conducted at different grade levels.)

Clarify comments. Much of what your participants say may need clarification; they need time—and your help—to formulate their responses clearly. Many times, participants do not say exactly what they mean, or they offer what appear to be superficial comments. By asking one or more follow-up questions, you help students articulate their ideas more clearly. If you do not understand a comment or if you notice puzzled looks, then ask the speaker to elaborate on the initial statement or to repeat it in different words: "Miyako, what do you mean when you say Jack needs adventure?" Question any special use of language, especially clichés or slang that other students may not find familiar:

Tanisha: I think Jack's getting smarter, too. And it seems like he's enjoying himself—fooling the giant and his wife, taking the harp right from under their noses— it's like a game for him.

Leader: Tanisha, how can something as scary as tricking a boy-eating ogre become a kind of game for Jack?

This effort to clarify is essential to good discussion, and your participants will soon grow comfortable with it. They will come to understand that you want to clarify their ideas because you are genuinely interested in exploring them.

Get support for opinions. Not all opinions offered during your discussion will be equally valid. Some opinions will be better substantiated by evidence from the selection than others. By asking students to recall or read relevant passages that support what they say, you encourage more attentive reading and help ensure that discussion is closely tied to the text. Thus, if a student asserts that "Jack is greedy," you might ask, "Sulema, what in the story makes you think that Jack is greedy?" Often, you will want to ask how or why the evidence supports the participant's opinion. If Sulema answers, "It says here, 'Jack was not content,'" you might ask, "Why does 'not content' make you think Jack is greedy?" Simply reading from the text is not providing evidence. Students should explain how the passage supports their idea:

 *Dialogue*

Jennifer: I think Jack got smarter each time he went to the giant's. It says, starting on page 154, that "this time he knew better than to go straight to the ogre's house. And when he got near it he waited behind a bush till he saw the ogre's wife come out with a pail to get some water, and then he crept into the house and got into the copper."

Leader: How does that show that Jack is getting smarter?

Jennifer: It shows he's planning.

Solicit additional opinions. Get your participants involved by asking them whether they agree or disagree with a comment under consideration. Ask, "Aaron, do you agree with Jennifer's point that . . . ?" or "Eric, how would you answer the question I just asked Shantel?" Then follow up on the answers they give. Students may offer the same opinion but have different reasons and different evidence for it. Such differences may indicate new avenues for exploration.

When you ask students for additional opinions, your task is not merely to add them to the discussion. Give your discussion continuity and coherence by asking questions that help your students see the relationships among ideas. Highlight possible connections between opinions your students have expressed. Ask, "Jason, is what you just said different from what Jaime said, that . . . ?" Or, "Shantel, are you agreeing with Jason's point that . . . ?" After a new idea has been explained, try to ask a question to link it back to earlier comments:

Dialogue

Leader: "Devin, is your idea that Jack climbed up the third time to get more money different from Rasheed's idea that Jack just wanted to take care of his mother?"

Develop ideas. Your students may fail to see all the consequences of their own thinking. If you feel that an idea expressed in discussion has important implications, draw them out with a follow-up question. In the following exchange, the leader is trying to get at the train of thought behind an interpretation:

Dialogue

Tiara: Jack has all the money he could possibly want from the hen, so what's left for him to do except hang around the house with his mother? He can't do that forever. He needs to do something, take a few risks, or else he will get bored. It was exciting the first two times up the beanstalk and so he went back to have an adventure.

Leader: Tiara, are you saying that Jack takes this risky third trip because he is looking for kicks or because having adventures is a necessary part of growing up?

The leader put options in the follow-up question both because she was unsure of what Tiara was implying and she wanted to avoid the appearance of signaling answers. By pursuing the implications of what your participants say, you help them enlarge and clarify their opinions. And, in the process, you uncover more ideas for your group to consider.

Test ideas. The most satisfying interpretations of a selection are those that account for all the relevant facts. It is a good idea, therefore, to have your participants consider evidence that might contradict their opinions or require them to modify their positions. Often, a version of one of your cluster questions can be helpful in getting a student to consider a relevant detail:

Leader: Lori, why does Jack succeed in this story?

Lori: It's all luck. Good things just happen to Jack.

Leader: If it's all luck, why does the author refer to Jack as "sharp as a needle"?

There is no intent here to prove the student's response wrong. By inquiring into the validity of an answer, the leader is only helping the participant think about whether an idea is consistent with all the evidence in the text. In response to the leader's follow-up question, Lori might say, "He's being sarcastic. Jack isn't sharp, he's dumb. The author is making fun of Jack." Here, the leader's follow-up question has uncovered more fully the student's point of view. By testing interpretations, you help your participants develop the flexibility to expand upon or reconsider their initial assumptions and judgments.

Distinguish among answers to the basic question.
As leader, your aim is to elicit your participants' ideas and opinions about your basic question. At any given moment in discussion, there are usually more good ideas expressed than you can work with at one time. Two participants may state opinions, one right after another, or one participant may offer a response with two good ideas in it, both worth pursuing. Decide which idea to pursue—keeping in mind both your basic question and your group's need for coherence in discussion—and then ask follow-up questions that build relationships between the new idea and those already offered. Your preparation and your cluster questions will help you. To make sure you don't forget ideas that you may want to pursue later, and to assure participants that their thoughts will not be lost or forgotten, jot them down on your seating chart. When you return to an idea, let your group hear you thinking out loud about the relationships you notice: "Miguel said earlier . . ."

※ ※ ※

Follow-up questions don't have to be perfectly worded. If your question is not clear, your students will let you know, and you can then rephrase it or try another. Take your time in thinking of questions, and concentrate on what your participants are saying. You do not have to follow up on every idea; experienced leaders generally ask one follow-up question for every two or three of their participants' responses. The important thing is to develop a habit of listening carefully and following up with questions. You will know you are doing an effective job of asking follow-up questions when you begin to hear your students asking each other for clarification and evidence in discussion.

Asking Follow-up Questions

EXERCISE FOR "A GAME OF CATCH"

Each of the following sequences consists of a leader's question and a participant's response. For each sequence, write a follow-up question you would ask, taking into account both the participant's response and the leader's question.

1. **Leader:** According to the story, do Glennie and Monk treat Scho unfairly?

   Participant: No, on the whole they behave very well toward a pushy kid.

   Your Follow-up Question:

2. **Leader:** Why do Monk and Glennie ignore what Scho says after he finds a seat in the tree?

   Participant: What did Scho say?

   Your Follow-up Question:

3. **Leader:** Why does Monk begin to throw the ball to Glennie once or twice before he gives Scho his grounder?

   Participant: Because Scho failed to catch one of the balls that Monk threw him.

   Your Follow-up Question:

4. **Leader:** *Just before Scho falls, why is his voice both "exuberant and panicky"?*

   Participant: *I don't think I could have those two feelings at the same time.*

   Your Follow-up Question:

5. **Leader:** *Why does Scho enlarge the scope of his game at the end of the story?*

   Participant: *I don't know.*

   Your Follow-up Question:

6. **Leader:** *Why does Scho tease the boys mainly while he is in the tree?*

   Participant 1: *Playing his game from the tree gives Scho a false sense of power because he is looking down on Glennie and Monk.*

   Participant 2: *Scho feels safe from any attempt Glennie and Monk make to shut him up.*

   Your Follow-up Question:

Questions from the Field

Last week, my students stumped me by all coming up with the same answer to my basic question. How do I generate a good discussion if there's no disagreement in my group?

Disagreement is not a goal of Shared Inquiry Discussion but a tool you can use to help your group fully explore a text's meaning. Even if your students seem frustratingly like-minded, you can still lead a fine discussion by using follow-up questions to identify shades of difference among their responses. Almost certainly, as students explain their ideas and look more closely at the text, they will discover areas in which their interpretations differ or hear ideas that they had not thought of before.

For example, in a discussion of "Jack and the Beanstalk," you might begin with the basic question *According to the story, is Jack's success due more to luck and magic or to his own abilities?* If the first few students respond by answering "his own abilities" and you follow up just by asking if anyone agrees or disagrees, it may take a fairly confident participant to speak out against what seems to be a unanimous view.

Instead, see if you can open up possible differences by asking one of the first few students a follow-up question, such as "What are the abilities that help Jack succeed?" Or, "Do you mean his physical abilities or his mental abilities?" Or, "Do his abilities help him take advantage of the luck and magic?" Asking one student to develop his or her initial answer will often help others discover areas in which their interpretations differ.

Asking for evidence is another way to help students discover differences between individual responses. Students may agree that Jack's success is due more to luck and magic but may use different evidence to support their claim. One might say Jack was lucky that "the man spoke truth after all" in telling Jack that the beans would "grow right up to the sky," prompting another student to say that Jack was even luckier when the ogre's wife "bundled Jack into the oven just as the ogre came in." You could then ask either of them, "Which place in the story had more to do with Jack's success?"

You can also help your participants identify their differences and think more deeply about the story if you are clear about what you are asking them to agree or disagree with during discussion. For example, suppose Yvonne says, "I think Jack's success is due more to his physical abilities. Even if he was lucky enough to trade for magic beans and smart enough to be nice to the ogre's wife, he wouldn't have been able to get the gold unless he was able to climb the beanstalk in the first place." If you follow up by asking, "Joshua, do you agree?", Joshua might simply nod his head because he does not know which part of Yvonne's idea you want him to address. But if you ask him to comment on a specific part of her response, such as, "Joshua, do you agree that Jack's success was due more to his physical abilities?", Joshua might say, "No, I think it was more because he was smart enough to know that if he didn't cut down the beanstalk when he did, the ogre would have eaten him and then Jack wouldn't have had any success anymore."

TEXTUAL ANALYSIS: HELPING YOUR GROUP EXAMINE A PASSAGE IN DETAIL

In textual analysis, a group discusses a single passage line by line, and sometimes word by word, raising questions about its meaning. Textual analysis should be a regular part of Shared Inquiry. You may do it any time the group's attention is focused on a specific passage. The following steps outline how to conduct textual analysis with your students.

When students are having an especially hard time with a text, textual analysis can help them get a foothold.

1. *Choose a passage.* Ask students which passage they are having difficulty with, or choose a passage yourself that seems important and challenging. Good possibilities for textual analysis are the beginning or ending of a selection, a crisis or a change of direction, or paragraphs that contain words and phrases the author seems to use in a special way. Your Teacher's Edition or Leader's Guide directs you to such passages.

2. *Read the passage aloud.* Ask someone to read the passage aloud, if it is short, while the others follow in their books. Having the passage read aloud focuses attention and may help some participants begin to understand what the passage means.

3. *Ask questions to help the group review the context.* For a story, ask who is speaking in the passage— the author, a narrator, or a character—and recall what incidents have occurred up to that point. For nonfiction, ask about the position of the passage in the argument as a whole. If the passage is at the beginning, does it introduce key terms or state the author's purpose? Does it describe a problem the author hopes to solve?

4. *Conduct a close reading.* Reread the passage line by line, asking questions you have prepared or that appear in your Teacher's Edition or Leader's Guide.

Discuss any word, phrase, or sentence that puzzles or interests you or your participants. Essentially, you are brainstorming ideas about what the passage might mean. Untangle difficult sentences by asking about separate clauses or phrases. Work on difficult words by asking questions about their meaning in context and letting students contribute their own or dictionary definitions. Invite your group to consider the author's specific choice of words with questions such as, "Why did the author select this particular way to say it?" Examine metaphors by asking about the comparisons they set up and their implications. While doing all this, try to remain open to all possibilities of meaning. Because every word in the story represents a decision the author has made, assume for the moment that everything might have importance in your understanding of the whole.

5. *Encourage participants to ask and answer questions.* Have students contribute questions and answer each other's questions, if they can. Not all of their questions will be useful. Some may have factual answers that the group will readily supply. Others will have no answer at all in the text. In the process of asking questions, though, your students may uncover new and significant interpretive problems. Allow the group to discuss these briefly. If they seem interesting, write them down so you can go back to them after you have worked through the whole passage.

When the passage has been examined, ask participants if they can relate any new discoveries to what has already been discussed, returning to one of the more interesting questions raised during textual analysis. The leader's notes on the following passage from "A Game of Catch" indicate the kinds of questions that could be raised in textual analysis.

The Teacher's Edition suggests that the passage beginning, "I got an idea," and ending, "with a fraction of a grin" is a good source for textual analysis.

• A GAME OF CATCH •

"I got an idea," said Glennie. "Why don't Monk and I catch for five minutes more, and then you can borrow one of our gloves?"

"That's all right with me," said Monk. He socked his fist into his mitt, and Glennie burned one in.

"All right," Scho said, and went over and sat under the tree. There in the shade he watched them resume their skillful play. They threw lazily fast or lazily slow—high, low, or wide—and always handsomely, their expressions serene, changeless, and forgetful. When Monk missed a low backhand catch, he walked indolently after the ball and, hardly even looking, flung it sidearm for an imaginary put-out. After a good while of this, Scho said, "Isn't it five minutes yet?"

"One minute to go," said Monk, with a fraction of a grin.

Scho stood up and watched the ball slap back and forth for several minutes more, and then he turned and pulled himself up into the crotch of the tree.

"Where are you going?" Monk asked.

"Just up the tree," Scho said.

"I guess he doesn't want to catch," said Monk.

Scho went up and up through the fat light-gray branches until they grew slender and bright and gave under him. He found a place where several supple branches were knit to make a dangerous chair, and sat there with his head coming out of the leaves into the sunlight. He could see the two other boys down below, the ball going back and forth between them as if they

3

Are they sincere?

Why lazily?

Forgetful of what? Scho? Is this an excuse?

Why does he grin? What is he feeling?

Why does Monk ask? Does he feel guilty?

Why does he choose a dangerous seat?

Why say this? Why doesn't Scho reply? Why doesn't Glennie say anything?

CLOSING THE DISCUSSION

By the end of Shared Inquiry Discussion, you want students to have heard and discussed a number of answers to your basic interpretive question, and all participants to be able to give their own answers and support them with evidence from the text. Because basic questions can have several satisfactory answers, members of your group will likely end up with different opinions. Having thoroughly discussed an interpretive question does not imply reaching total agreement, or even a majority opinion, about how best to answer it.

When you feel the basic question has been thoroughly examined, you have reached a point of resolution. Before going on to a new question, try to uncover any answers to the basic question that have not yet been offered in discussion, and encourage students to determine whether each of them has arrived at a satisfactory answer. Then, if you have more time, ask another basic question to begin discussion of a new topic.

If time for discussion has come to an end, you can close discussion in one of the following ways:

■ *Ask students to repeat answers they have heard.* As students recall answers to the basic question, they recognize what interpretations have evolved as well as what might be discussed further. Often new ideas are discovered.

■ *Have participants look back at their original written answers.* Often, students find that their opinions have changed during discussion. Ask if anyone had an answer that was not discussed. You might also use this time to call on members of the group who did not participate very much: "Jessica, did you hear an answer that made sense to you?" After your participants review the answers they remember, check your chart for any additional answers and ask participants about them: "Bill, didn't you have a different answer, something about . . . ?" Or, "Eric, what was that other point you made about . . . ?"

■ *Encourage students to record their final answers to the basic question.* They might write their answers down in a Junior Great Books notebook or complete the Building Your Answer activity page. Ask students to take into account their earlier written response as well as the opinions and evidence offered by others during discussion. This synthesis occurs naturally throughout Shared Inquiry Discussion, but now is the time to emphasize that even the most confidently held opinions can be improved by the ideas of others. Ask if anyone arrived at an answer that differs substantially from the one that he or she wrote down at the start of discussion. Then ask those participants who changed their minds to identify the ideas that seemed especially persuasive.

* * *

Shared Inquiry is a thinking process that does not necessarily end when discussion time is up. In fact, having successful discussions should inspire further reflection. Writing after discussion is one of the ways you can encourage your participants to continue their interpretive work on a selection.

CLASSROOM MANAGEMENT Tip

PLANNING DISCUSSION TIME

If you have block scheduling, allow 45 minutes to an hour for Shared Inquiry Discussion. With a group of 15–20 students, you need at least 30 minutes to allow each student to participate, but 45 minutes to an hour will allow for more in-depth exploration and time for students to raise their own questions and concerns. This longer time frame is also important if your average class size is more than 20 students.

Although the amount of time allotted for discussion might be dictated by a predetermined length for class or activity periods or for lunch, don't try to squeeze your discussion into less than 30 minutes. It isn't conducive to the reflective nature of Shared Inquiry Discussion.

Although an hour may be too long for younger students to stay focused on interpretive discussion, scheduling that much time will allow you to work with smaller groups of about 10 students while other students work on another activity such as art.

SHARING QUESTIONS DISCUSSION: A VARIANT FOR READ-ALOUD PARTICIPANTS

For participants in the Read-Aloud program, we recommend Sharing Questions Discussion—an adaptation of Shared Inquiry Discussion.

Rather than beginning discussion with a basic interpretive question, open Sharing Questions Discussion by writing five or six interpretive questions on the board or on chart paper, in the order you intend to ask them. Seeing the questions will help students follow the discussion and focus on each question as it is being discussed. Then read the first question aloud and ask for answers, making sure students understand that it is an interpretive question and that more than one answer is possible. After a few answers are given, foster the exchange of opinions by asking individual children if they agree or disagree with what they have heard, and try to develop a few strong answers.

As in Shared Inquiry Discussion, you should encourage students to support their answers by referring to the text. Children need not read a passage in order to substantiate their opinions—recalling a line or a part of the text and paraphrasing it for the group is perfectly acceptable. However, if students have difficulty citing evidence, reread the passage you think they have in mind, and ask whether it supports their answer. Modeling this return to the text should quickly get them in the habit of referring to the story themselves. As their listening and reading skills develop, so will their ability to find and cite evidence on their own.

The phrasing of your follow-up questions may also help young students recall story details more easily. For example, for the Read-Aloud selection "The King of the Frogs," instead of asking a student, "What in the story makes you think Mmumi was angry?" ask, "What does Mmumi say or do that makes you think he was angry?" The phrase "say or do" is more specific and helps students understand what constitutes evidence.

After children have given a number of responses, ask them whether they have each heard an answer that satisfies them. If some students indicate that they are not yet satisfied, have them contribute additional answers at this time. Then proceed to the next question.

Do not hesitate to ask students questions to clarify their answers, draw out implications, or test the consistency of their answers. Although students may not always be able to answer your questions, hearing them helps students learn the characteristics of reflective thinking and clear communication. Conclude Sharing Questions Discussion by reiterating that all the opinions offered helped everyone understand the story or poem better.

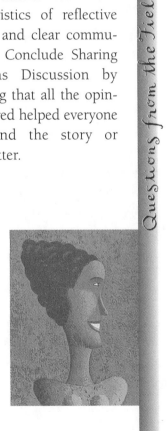

Questions from the Field

Shared Inquiry Discussion will be a new experience for my students. How do I help them understand what discussion is all about?

Participants in Junior Great Books will have a clearer idea of what is expected of them if, from time to time, you guide them in assessing how well they listened and responded to each other during Shared Inquiry Discussion. They will also value the activity more when they pause to consider how their own thinking has developed over the course of discussion. Did they strive to resolve the story's important interpretive problems? Did they consider others' answers? Did they weigh the evidence in support of each possibility?

After Shared Inquiry Discussion, call attention to the times when a tentatively offered opinion triggered an important insight for someone else. Illustrate how certain ideas were reevaluated and developed. Remind participants that in discussion many ideas are put forward and that it's necessary to be open to change if the evidence demands it.

A good sign that participants are starting to feel comfortable with Shared Inquiry Discussion is that they no longer respond exclusively to you—they talk directly to each other. They help each other out, suggesting relevant evidence or lines of reasoning to support answers. Perhaps they will even anticipate some of your follow-up questions by asking fellow participants for clarification or evidence. When participants see that they can contribute to Shared Inquiry Discussion by working with others' ideas as well as their own, they will become more attentive listeners and more active readers and thinkers.

Chapter Highlight

Dividing Your Class for Discussion

Shared Inquiry Discussion should be an intensive experience for students, with many opportunities to participate. A group of about 15 students allows for both diverse opinions and repeated involvement. But how do you divide full-size classes into manageable discussion groups? Here are some ideas we have collected from teachers.

ASSIGN HALF THE CLASS TO AN INDEPENDENT OR SMALL-GROUP ACTIVITY.

Independent seat work or paired activities will keep students productively occupied while you lead others in discussion. You can ask students to work on Junior Great Books activities. Or, if you have a self-contained classroom, you can juggle this time between Junior Great Books and another subject.

Students who have already participated in discussion can work on the Junior Great Books writing activities, complete the Building Your Answer activity page, or read the next story and write questions for the Sharing Questions activity. Students in the second discussion group can complete activity pages for the Junior Great Books unit. Listening to audiotapes of the next story can be engrossing for younger students. It helps to assign the second group a piece with a due date. If you give students routine assignments or ones that they have already successfully begun, rather than unfamiliar or difficult tasks, they will have less of a need to interrupt you.

SEND HALF THE CLASS TO ANOTHER ROOM.

Pair your discussion time with other half-class activities such as computer lab or library period. Or arrange with another teacher to trade times during which half the class may join the other teacher's class for work in another subject area, a period of study, sustained silent reading, or reading aloud. One or more colleagues teaching the same grade can work out a mutually helpful schedule.

ARRANGE FOR ANOTHER TRAINED LEADER TO TAKE ONE GROUP WHILE YOU LEAD THE OTHER.

This task is manageable for parent volunteers. Try to recruit a few volunteers who can commit to steady involvement.

Your school might also designate a Junior Great Books site coordinator to lead discussions in several classrooms weekly. We've seen a resource teacher, gifted or federal programs teacher, librarian, teacher aide, guidance counselor, and assistant principal take on this role and love it. Keep in mind that anyone who will be leading discussion needs to complete the Basic Leader Training Course.

Your leader-partner can also work with you to prepare interpretive questions. Try to alternate groups between the two of you, so that you can keep track of how all your students are doing.

When two groups discuss at the same time, it is easier for everyone to concentrate on discussion if each group has its own space. While one group is in the classroom, the other might be in the library, resource room, lounge, or hallway.

INVOLVE HALF THE CLASS AS OBSERVERS OF THE DISCUSSION.

The key idea here is "involve." Give the observers a real job to do. One third-grade teacher has observers write questions they would like to ask participants. Halfway through and at the end of discussion, observers can bring up their issues during a question time. Another teacher asks observers to prepare to "help out" ideas they like by bringing up additional evidence and reasons near the end of discussion.

If you use this arrangement, structure the discussion to facilitate observation. Arrange students in an inner circle of discussion participants and an outer circle of observers, where everyone can see each other. Plan for time during or after discussion for the observers to present their questions or statements.

Chapter Review

1. Arrange the classroom seating in a circle or square to make the room more conducive to Shared Inquiry Discussion. In this arrangement, all students can see and hear each other better. Make sure students also have a flat surface on which to place their books and write their answers.

2. Make sure students know and understand the four rules of Shared Inquiry Discussion.

3. Use a seating chart to help you keep track of students' comments during discussion and to make sure all students have a chance to participate during discussion.

4. Begin discussion with an interpretive question. Give participants time to write it down and to write their answers. For younger students, put the questions you are going to ask in discussion on the board or on chart paper.

5. Conduct discussion by asking questions that prompt thoughtful inquiry, elicit evidence in support of answers, and maintain the interpretive focus of discussion. During discussion

   - Ask follow-up questions often.
   - Turn to the text frequently.
   - Be persistent in striving for answers to your basic question.
   - Be patient with participants.
   - Encourage students to speak directly to each other.
   - Be open to challenges to any assumptions in your questions.
   - Give everyone a chance to contribute.

6. Close discussion by reviewing the answers the group has developed. Closing discussion does not mean the group has come to a consensus about the answer to the basic question. Rather, various students have developed good answers that satisfy their quest for a better understanding of the text.

Chapter 4

CONDUCTING THE

JUNIOR GREAT BOOKS

INTERPRETIVE ACTIVITIES

$\mathcal{S}$hared Inquiry Discussion, with its focus on interpretive questions, reflection, and sharing, typifies Shared Inquiry, but it is only one part of the process of interpretive reading and discussion. For students to successfully interpret what they read, they must establish a literal understanding of the selection—they need to know who the characters are, what the sequence of events is, and what the important words mean. However, they don't need to thoroughly master the facts before beginning to look at the interpretive issues of a selection.

The Junior Great Books interpretive activities support students, at every level, in the interpretive reading process. Each activity has a distinct purpose and rhythm. Some activities are intended to prepare students to bring their prior knowledge to bear on the story. Others will help them pursue issues they considered during their reading and assess their reactions. You will achieve the best results—and your students will enjoy the variety of the activities more—if you keep each activity's objective in mind as you conduct it. This chapter will give you suggestions for conducting the activities at all grade levels. You can find complete instructions for conducting the interpretive activities in your Teacher's Edition or Leader's Guide.

> Shared Inquiry is more than discussion. It's also a process of building comprehension through open-ended activities.

To conduct the interpretive activities, you should prepare as you would for Shared Inquiry Discussion—read the selection twice, take notes, and write interpretive questions that interest you. In addition, you should read through the unit's activities and think about your own responses to the prompts. However, you may want to reserve creating your basic question and cluster of interpretive questions for Shared Inquiry Discussion until after you have heard your students' questions. Then you'll have the opportunity to incorporate some of their questions into the discussion.

Don't underestimate the importance of your own curiosity about the meaning of the selection as a motivating force for your students. The model you present to students—someone intellectually engaged with literature, asking interpretive questions, organizing ideas, and searching for answers—is probably the most important teaching strategy in the Shared Inquiry approach to learning. Your attitude toward the process will also be reflected in your students' attitudes. Keeping your outlook positive and focusing on what the group wants to explore can make the difference between students who are motivated to find out answers for themselves and those who think the task is beyond their abilities.

PREREADING ACTIVITIES

The prereading activity provides a starting point for the interpretive work on a selection. It either anticipates one of the interpretive issues of a selection or helps students overcome potential obstacles to understanding. Since this activity is meant to provide students with an orientation as they begin work on a selection, you should keep it brief.

INTRODUCTION (GRADES K–2)

Your Teacher's Edition provides brief introductions that are meant to orient your students or provide necessary definitions or references. To meet the needs of your class, you might have to add to the recommended introduction by bringing in pictures or other visual aids to help students visualize the story as you read aloud to them. However, we suggest that you keep the introduction brief, so that you don't diminish the anticipation of the first reading.

TEXT OPENER (GRADES 3–6)

Introduce the Text Opener as suggested in your Teacher's Edition and go over the activity page, if one is provided. Students can answer the questions in writing before sharing answers, or they can discuss the questions as a class. During sharing, encourage students to include the reasoning behind their answers. Be prepared to hear a wide variety of ideas and responses. Text Openers should generally last only 5–10 minutes. When you sense that students have grasped the ideas behind the activity, bring it to a close.

At the conclusion of the first reading, ask the question given at the end of the story in your Teacher's Edition. Spending a few moments on this question will help students connect the work they did in the Text Opener to their understanding of the story.

PREREADING QUESTIONS (GRADES 7–12)

Choose, or have students choose, a prereading question from the list provided in your Leader's Guide. Have students write briefly before sharing their answers with the class. Alternatively, you can hold a brief discussion (10–20 minutes) on the question of your choice. In some cases, you may want students to research historical or cultural information and share what they have found with other members of the group.

Most students will have a number of ideas to write down immediately in response to the prereading question, and you should encourage your students to record their initial thoughts and opinions freely. However, you can help students elaborate on their answers by suggesting that they ask themselves the following questions (you may want to give students these questions in a handout to refer to as they write):

> *Is there a word or phrase in the prereading question that needs to be explained or defined?*
>
> *Is there some personal experience or a more general example that you would like to use to illustrate your answer?*

MULTIPLE READINGS

The multiple readings that are stressed in Junior Great Books present the perfect opportunity to employ various reading strategies. A good way to help students begin the work of interpreting a challenging text is to read the selection aloud to them. We recommend reading aloud not only for the primary grades, but also for older students. This practice lets students concentrate on the story itself rather than the mechanics of reading and helps them fix the plot in their

Questions from the Field

Shouldn't I tell my students about the author before they read the story?

You can, but we don't recommend it for several reasons. First, the information given in brief biographical accounts of authors is generally of little use in developing a well-supported interpretation of a story. Second, when you provide biographical information about the author, you are stepping out of your role as leader, a co-learner in Shared Inquiry. As a result, students may misunderstand why you are giving them "answers" about the author and might very well think that you're telling them "why" the author wrote the story. Third, the facts you provide about the author may lead discussion away from the story, when the purpose of Shared Inquiry is to come to a better understanding of the text itself.

Of course, students occasionally need help in establishing a context for the work they are about to read. Text Openers (Series 3–6) and prereading questions (Series 7–9) are designed specifically for this purpose. For example, one of the prereading questions suggested for "Anne Frank: Diary of a Young Girl" (Series 7) is *What happened to the Jews in Europe during World War II?* Having students research the answer to this question, or just asking students to share what they already know about the subject with those who are not sure, will increase students' understanding and appreciation of the selection without compromising your role as Shared Inquiry leader. Other prereading questions for the Anne Frank selection include *How would you feel if you were not allowed to go outside for over two years, and no one could come to see you?* and *How would you keep your spirits up in a time of terrible hardship?* These questions allow students to reflect on their own experiences and opinions about situations similar to those described in Anne's diary. Answering these questions, even briefly, will help students to think more deeply about the text itself and learn from it by comparing it to their experiences.

In general, historical or cultural information, rather than author information, is needed to put a selection into perspective. In this case, the Text Opener or an optional World of the Story activity will provide students with the background information needed to interpret the story. For example, both the Text Opener and the World of the Story activity for "Soumchi" (Series 6, First Semester) give students pertinent facts about Israel during the 1940s, the setting of the story. Such information helps students understand the action of the story and is far more useful to them than hearing details about the author's life.

It is still best to keep new information to a minimum before the first reading, so that students are not overwhelmed with trying to digest a lot of factual material and reflect on interpretive issues at the same time. In addition, providing too much information before discussion can make students passive and can obscure many fruitful lines of inquiry that could fuel an interpretive discussion or motivate a research project.

minds. It also gives students confidence in their ability to understand the language and ideas of the story when they return to it for a second reading and note taking. Even high school students can benefit from oral readings. Listening as you read the selection aloud helps students pick up challenging vocabulary in context, comprehend difficult sentence structure, and gain a sense of the author's style.

See Questions from the Field, p. 104.

While reading to your students, do not ask prediction questions.* Such questions lead students to guess what the author will say next, and in Shared Inquiry, students are encouraged not to speculate but to base their opinions on the text. Moreover, Junior Great Books selections are chosen for their discussibility—the interpretive problems that they present. It is often the unpredictable nature of a story or essay that makes it discussible, so asking students to make predictions about this type of material will only frustrate them.

GRADES K–1

Unless your students in the Read-Aloud program are strong readers, they should not have the books in front of them or try to follow along on the first reading. Instead, read expressively and have students listen to get an overall sense of the story. Keep interruptions during your first reading to a minimum. (Since we recommend three readings of the selection at this age, students will have ample time to catch up on details later.) You can quickly gloss difficult words by using the definitions given in your Teacher's Edition.

On second and third readings, it is preferable to have students follow along while someone reads to them. Once they have a sense of the story, following along and joining in reading the underlined passages helps young children build their sight vocabularies. The audiotapes available for each Read-Aloud series can help you ensure that students have several opportunities to hear the stories read aloud.

GRADES 2–6

Once students are able to read, they should be encouraged to follow along in their books while you read the story aloud to them. Listening to the story read aloud helps students derive meanings of words through context, recognize the author's tone, and hear the pronunciation of unfamiliar words. As students follow along, encourage them to mark words that are new to them and things that they do not understand. Keep interruptions to a minimum during your first reading. Definitions of difficult and unusual words are provided in your Teacher's Edition and can be quickly supplied to students while you are reading.

The second reading in Junior Great Books Series 2–6, done in conjunction with note taking, can be conducted in a number of ways. You may choose to read aloud to students while they follow along in their books, have them read independently while they take notes, have them read round-robin style while taking and sharing notes, or have them work together in pairs or small groups. The audiotapes for Junior Great Books Series 2–6 can help you provide support for weaker readers and add variety to the reading routine.

GRADES 7–12

Hearing the story read aloud is also important in Junior Great Books Series 7–9 and Introduction to Great Books. However, students may prefer to read aloud themselves. If you choose to have students read aloud, let them become familiar with the selection first. Students are then better prepared to read it aloud to each other on the second reading.

You can assign the two readings in a variety of ways. However, you should emphasize a move toward more independent work. With nonfiction pieces, it is particularly important that students take notes during both the first and second readings of the selection.

Because the selections are challenging, even secondary school students can benefit from additional readings. Make sure students understand that reading a selection several times does not mean they are poor readers. Rather, it is an important strategy that good readers use when trying to improve their understanding of a complex work.

Questions from the Field

Why aren't prediction questions used in Junior Great Books?

Prediction questions are not a part of Junior Great Books because we believe that there are better, more genuine means of promoting students' active engagement with literature. We also believe that students' understanding of a story is more effectively aided through a questioning strategy—and a reading routine—that focuses on important questions of meaning.

When presented with a challenging work of literature, all good readers naturally wonder how the story will turn out, but it is their ability to move beyond the factual level that truly motivates their reading— and rereading—of a text. In Junior Great Books, students learn to connect personally with a text and formulate their own questions, through such activities as

the Text Opener and Sharing Questions; to read closely and actively through the Directed Notes activity and the open-ended G.B.'s questions in the Read-Aloud program; and to think about and develop answers to interpretive questions. It is these habits of questioning and reflection that sustain readers for the long haul— synthesizing the story's facts in order to form a personal, coherent interpretation of the story.

REFLECTING ON THE SELECTION BETWEEN READINGS

This activity allows students to explore their initial reactions by sharing their own questions about the story, and it will give you an opportunity to help students overcome obstacles to literal comprehension, to raise interpretive issues, and to gauge students' areas of interest in the selection.

SHARING FIRST RESPONSES AND "MY QUESTION" (GRADES K–1)

Although the sharing first responses activity parallels Sharing Questions in higher grades, it is not as ambitious an activity. Sharing first responses is meant primarily to introduce young students to one aspect of the interpretive reading process: noting personal reactions is important when trying to understand a text.

After the first reading, allow five minutes or so for sharing first responses. Students might not have any questions, but they will probably have some reactions. Always encourage students to voice their opinions by asking what parts of the story they especially liked and why. To clear up any confusion children might have about the story or poem, ask if they have any questions. (They will begin to ask questions on their own after they have participated in this activity a few times.) Answer, or have the class answer, the factual questions. If children ask interpretive questions, do not engage in a lengthy discussion. Students will be far better prepared to address such questions after they have heard the selection read a few more times. Instead, tell the class that you think an interpretive question has been asked and that they will want to think about it during the course of the week.

Read-Aloud Note

OPTIONS FOR SHARING ART

Visualizing an aspect of a story also helps students reflect on a selection. You may want to reassure children that you're not concerned about how well they draw—instead, you're looking forward to seeing the ideas they represent in their drawings. The share and compare component of the art activities is especially important for promoting the concept of different, individual interpretations. You may try any of the following ways of helping children share their art:

Small Groups If your children sit in small groups at tables, encourage them to explain their pictures to other students in the group. They can also explain their drawings to you as you visit the different tables.

Whole Class Have students take turns holding up their pictures before the whole class. Let them explain their drawings and take questions from other students.

Display Area Display artwork on a Junior Great Books bulletin board. Encourage students to compare their work with that of a classmate and ask each other about why they made different choices.

Young students often need to hear a complex story more than once before they understand it enough to form questions, so this activity will be brief. However, allowing students a few minutes to share their responses prompts them to reflect on what they have just heard. It also helps them establish the habit of thinking about how they are reacting to a story.

The "My Question" activity gives students a second opportunity to ask questions after hearing the story read at home. A sample letter in the appendix of your Teacher's Edition and the "Note to the At-Home Reader" in the front of each volume of the student anthologies give instructions about the "My Question" activity. Students write, or have someone write, their questions on the "My Question" activity page at the end of the unit. Students' questions do not have to be interpretive.

If students are unable to do the second reading, G.B.'s questions, and "My Question" at home, you can either conduct these at-home activities as another in-class session or have reading buddies help students with these activities. Reading buddies can be older students, volunteers, or resource teachers who work one-on-one with students.

The day after reading the selection with the at-home reader, have students cut out their questions and pin them on a Junior Great Books bulletin board. Tell students that they will be thinking about their questions during the next few days and discussing some of them in Sharing Questions Discussion. Encourage students to look at the questions during other activities to see if any questions are relevant.

SHARING QUESTIONS (GRADES 2-12)

Sharing Questions encourages students to value their own curiosity, and that of their classmates, and to use that curiosity to learn more about the selection. On a more practical level, Sharing Questions can help students by providing an opportunity to clear up misreadings and correct factual errors. After the first reading, urge students to ask about anything in the selection that they wondered about, such as why an event happened the way it did or why a character did or said a particular thing.

In Sharing Questions, students take responsibility for identifying gaps in their comprehension of a selection.

Try to incorporate students' questions into the activities for a unit. Whenever possible, use students' own wording of questions. You can also point out questions on the activity pages that are similar to ones asked by particular students. If any of the students' questions are related to the basic question you plan to lead in Shared Inquiry Discussion, you may be able to include some of them in your cluster.

You can lead Sharing Questions in several ways, as shown by the following four options. Keep in mind that however you choose to conduct the activity, Sharing Questions is primarily a time for students to voice their early curiosity about a story. To keep the activity focused and contained, do not spend too much time on any one question.

Option 1. Sharing Questions Orally

As a whole-class activity, invite students to share their questions informally for five minutes or so. Answer, or have the class answer, factual questions by referring to the relevant passages from the text. If students ask interpretive questions, which they will naturally do after they have completed a few units, do not engage in a lengthy discussion. Instead, entertain one or two answers to the question and say that it seems to be interpretive—students will want to think more about it during the course of the unit.

JUNIOR GREAT BOOKS BULLETIN BOARD

A simple way to help students keep track of their work over the course of a unit is to dedicate one of the bulletin boards in your classroom to Junior Great Books. You can display students' questions, interpretive drawings, and writing assignments on the board. Each time you begin a new unit, you may want to add the title of the story to the Junior Great Books bulletin board in a style that reflects the tone, setting, characters, or author of the story.

Option 2. Putting Questions on a Junior Great Books Bulletin Board

Students can work independently, writing down any questions they have. These questions can then be posted on a bulletin board reserved for Junior Great Books work. Another variation is to copy all or some of the questions onto a handout for students to keep in a Junior Great Books notebook. Have students look over the list of questions, and suggest that they start thinking about one they would like to answer. In this way, students can use the questions to aid their reflection on the story. As students complete subsequent activities throughout the week, they can add questions to the board.

Option 3. Sharing Questions in Small Groups

As a small-group activity, have each student contribute one question to a group list. Or, have the group generate several questions while working together. Collect the lists and photocopy them for distribution, or have the whole class briefly discuss one or two questions from each list.

Option 4. Making a Class List of Questions

A more structured, whole-class variation of Sharing Questions is having students offer their questions while you record them on the board or on chart paper. Clarify their questions if necessary, and include the name of the student who contributed the question. After you have collected six or eight questions, have the class suggest and briefly consider answers to each one. As you do so, help students understand the difference between factual and interpretive questions by providing brief definitions: factual questions have only one correct answer based on the story, and interpretive questions have more than one good answer that can be supported by details in the story.

Sometimes a question cannot be answered with evidence from the text. When this happens, collect one or two brief responses and then point out to the class that their answers were about things not in the story—there is no information provided in the story to answer that question satisfactorily. Because the success of this version of Sharing Questions depends on your ability to see the interpretive potential in students' questions, it is important to complete your own two readings and question writing first.

NOTE TAKING

Taking notes on a selection is a way for students to use writing to gain understanding. Not only does taking notes foster students' ability to recall evidence, it also encourages students to read more carefully and with greater attention to detail, and helps them begin to see connections, patterns, or other relationships present in the selection.

G.B.'s QUESTIONS AND AT-HOME QUESTIONS (GRADES K-2)

Before you send the books home, be sure students understand what they are to do. Ask students to follow along while being read to and, if they can, to repeat or join in saying any underlined phrases. In the Read-Aloud program, point to a picture of G.B. and tell children to pause whenever they see him and talk about their answer to the question in the box. Encourage children to mention the parts of the story that helped them think about their answer. (The sample letter in the appendix of your Teacher's Edition and the "Note to

Answering G.B.'s questions forms a basis for note-taking activities in later grades.

the At-Home Reader" in the front of each volume of the student anthologies will also help the parents or other adult partners understand their role in the process.)

G.B. does not appear in Junior Great Books Series 2 because second-grade students, who can read, should be better able to recognize the questions in the margins as the at-home questions without the help of a mascot. Ask students to listen as the at-home partner reads and to follow along as best they can. Tell them to pause and discuss the at-home questions in the margin. Point out to students those instances in which they will be asked to underline parts of the story.

Students using the Read-Aloud program and Junior Great Books Series 2 should be encouraged to share their responses to G.B.'s or the at-home questions during the third reading of the selection. When you do the third reading in class, have students follow along in their books. Pause when you come to the questions in the margins, and collect students' responses. When appropriate, use the questions printed in your Teacher's Edition to follow up on their answers.

DIRECTED NOTES (GRADES 3–9)

Explain the Directed Notes activity using the information provided in your Teacher's Edition or Leader's Guide. For the first few sessions, you may want to show students your own notes to help them understand how note taking is done. You may choose to give students class time to take their notes or have them do it as homework. Having students do the Directed Notes activity on a regular basis encourages them to read more carefully and pay greater attention to details, and helps to tie together elements throughout the selection.

Giving students class time to share their notes fosters their ability to recall details and use evidence, and provides practice in drawing inferences from the text. You don't need to have students share notes on the entire selection, particularly if it is a long story. For Series 3–6, the sample responses provided in your Teacher's Edition can help you identify pages on which a range and diversity of notes are possible. If some of your students have difficulty taking notes, sharing notes during class time allows them to hear the insights of their classmates. To assist students having difficulty, prompt them to take notes by asking if they have heard any notes that they agreed with or if what another student said sparked an idea. Consider the following options for having students share their notes:

Option 1. Sharing Notes as You Read Aloud
If your students are new to the activity, or are not fluent readers, you may want to have them follow along and mark their texts while you read the story aloud. Pause after every page or two to ask what they marked and why.

Option 2. Taking and Sharing Notes in Small Groups
Directed Notes can also be done in small, mixed-ability groups of three to five students who take turns reading aloud. Students can then share their notes with the whole class after the second reading is complete. Once your students become comfortable with this method of sharing notes, you might let them share their notes and reasons in the small group. Make sure students understand that the group need not agree on a note.

Option 3. Silent Reading Followed by Whole-Class Sharing
If your class is composed largely of independent readers, they can take notes during an independent, silent reading of the story. Later, they can share their notes during a whole-class activity. Begin by having students take turns reading the story aloud. Have them pause after each paragraph or two so that the class can share the different notes they have taken on those passages.

INTERPRETIVE NOTE SOURCE (HIGH SCHOOL)

In addition to using the interpretive note source, high school students should also write a word or two in the margin of the text explaining why they marked the passage as they did. Make students aware that because fiction and nonfiction present different kinds of reading challenges, the note-taking routines differ slightly.

Note taking for fiction. With fiction selections, the suggested interpretive note source is intended for the second reading, to develop students' thinking once they have grasped the basic plot of the story. On their first reading of a fiction selection, have students note whatever interests or puzzles them or seems important. Another possibility is to ask students to mark anything that reminds them of, or gives them a new perspective on, their prereading question.

Note taking for nonfiction. When students read nonfiction, they will encounter unfamiliar terms and abstract arguments, and they may feel that what should be an easy first step—reading the selection—is a stumbling block. For this reason, students should use an interpretive note source during the first reading of a nonfiction selection to help them organize their thoughts and follow the author's argument. You might also explain that philosophical writing often seems difficult at first because the author is trying to develop a new perspective on an old problem or is developing an original concept that involves complex and subtle ideas. Remind students that they are not being asked to accept the author's ideas as facts, but rather to understand them thoroughly and think about how they relate to the problem the author is addressing.

During the second reading of a nonfiction selection, have students use another interpretive note source, if one is provided. Or you may have students keep in mind several of their questions while reading. Tell them to mark anything the author says that addresses these questions, even if students disagree with the author's opinions. After the second reading, students can write answers to the questions they have considered.

Another good way to help students with nonfiction is to have them answer the following: What is the main question the author is trying to answer? Why is he or she interested in this question? Imagining that the author is writing in response to a question that he or she has posed can help students think about the essay and why the author thought the ideas were important.

INTERPRETING WORDS

Although Interpreting Words activities differ in procedure, a common element is the sharing of responses. Interpreting Words activities also lend themselves well to work in pairs or small groups. Even when the directions call for students to complete activity pages independently, allow time for the class to share answers. Doing so will achieve the primary purpose of the Interpreting Words activities: to give students practice in discovering how the meaning of an individual word or phrase contributes to the overall meaning of a story. The directions for Interpreting Words activities, provided in your Teacher's Edition or Leader's Guide, provide specific guidance in how to draw out students' thinking.

CLASSROOM MANAGEMENT Tip

NOTE TAKING IN STUDENT BOOKS

Taking notes in their books helps students interact directly with the selection and locate evidence more easily during discussion. The Great Books Foundation strives to keep the cost of materials low so that schools will be encouraged to let students keep their books. This allows students not only to take notes in the books but also to reread their favorite stories. However, for some schools, even with the low cost of the books, it's not possible to use the books as consumables.

If students cannot write in their books, they can easily mark the text with removable self-stick note papers. Teachers sometimes color-code the Directed Notes prompt, asking students to mark one choice with one color of note paper and the other choice with a different color. As students become more advanced in their note-taking skills, they should be encouraged to keep a journal to note their reactions to the story, their questions, and story events or ideas that seem important.

Chapter Highlight

Working with Challenging Vocabulary

Junior Great Books selections have not been simplified to meet a controlled vocabulary—the words appear exactly as the author or translator wrote them. Brief glosses for some words are provided in the Teacher's Editions for the younger grades so that teachers can give students quick definitions during the first reading. But because the selections contain an exceptionally broad range of vocabulary, students may need further help in dealing with unfamiliar words and with familiar words that are used in unfamiliar ways. When conducting your Junior Great Books program, there are a number of ways you can help students expand their vocabularies and learn strategies for understanding words that are new to them.

HAVE STUDENTS KEEP LISTS OF NEW WORDS THAT THEY FIND INTERESTING, UNUSUAL, OR HELPFUL.

Maintaining a list of words encourages students to add to their working vocabularies new words they encounter in literature. In the Read-Aloud program, students can list words on the "My Favorite Words" page at the end of each volume of their student anthologies. Older students can keep such lists in a Junior Great Books notebook or in a journal. Because students are selecting words they find appealing, they are apt to view this type of vocabulary work as fun rather than as a sign of a failure on their part.

LET STUDENTS RAISE QUESTIONS ABOUT WORDS THEY FIND UNUSUAL OR CONFUSING.

When helping students come to a better understanding of these words, it is important for you to distinguish words that are significant to the meaning of the selection from those that are less central. You may find yourself making these distinctions naturally during your preparation. Some words, whether unusual or fairly ordinary, will give you pause, and others, though perhaps more exotic, will not raise your curiosity. These words may help create the setting or mood of the story, but they don't figure in important interpretive issues in the work. Children will probably find, as you do, that these words are not essential to their understanding of the story and will read right over them, figuring out rough meanings from context. For example, when reading in "Cinderella" (Series 2, Second Semester) that the stepsisters had "rooms with parquet floors" or that Cinderella "coiffed them to perfection" rather than leave her stepsisters' hair "in a tangle," children will gather that *parquet* is fancy flooring and *coiffed* is related to having nicely styled hair. Instead of explaining these words, give students the opportunity to raise questions about them after the first reading. This approach allows you to see just which words captured students' attention and lets you help students get answers for themselves. You can direct students to look at the words in the context of the passages in which they appear, have another student give the definition, or send students to a dictionary.

ASK QUESTIONS THAT GUIDE STUDENTS TO SEARCH THE CONTEXT FOR CLUES TO A WORD'S MEANING.

This activity, done prior to discussion, is the best way for students to grasp less significant vocabulary. Asking participants to memorize definitions for a long list of words chosen randomly from the selection will only deflect them from their search for meaning in the story as a whole. Besides, by removing the words from context, you remove the students' impetus for learning them.

WORK WITH SIGNIFICANT VOCABULARY JUST AS YOU WOULD ANY OTHER INTERPRETIVE PROBLEM.

Unfamiliar words that seem directly related to problems of meaning will be more important in thinking about a selection. In your preparation, you will have noted words that seem especially intriguing and important, and you may have written questions about them. In addition, your students' own ideas about the story might lead them to ask about or comment on words that had not caught your attention but seem to deserve the group's careful thought. Sharing students' questions in class after the first reading gives participants an opportunity to bring up these words and begin thinking about them.

Chapter Highlight Cont.

Even seemingly commonplace words, such as *beautiful* in "Cinderella," may carry a great weight of meaning within a given work. This is especially true of the Introduction to Great Books selections. For example, the Declaration of Independence (Introduction to Great Books Second Series) abounds with long words such as *annihilation, consanguinity,* and *usurpation,* but a more fruitful discussion might center on interpreting the full significance of the seemingly simple *one people* or *right.*

During Shared Inquiry Discussion, deal with significant words as you would any point needing clarification. First, ask for a rough definition—a participant's own or a dictionary definition (the rules of discussion do not permit you to offer one). Then, in follow-up questions, inquire about the word's connotations in context and the author's possible reasons for using that particular word rather than another. Guide participants to relate what is said about the word to the interpretive question being discussed. In this way, they will see how the meaning of a word both derives from and contributes to the context in which it is used.

✳ ✳ ✳

As your students come to see that an interpretation can turn on the possible meanings of a single word, their interest in exploring unfamiliar vocabulary will grow. In time, handling new words will become a natural and regular part of their effort to understand what they read.

SHARED INQUIRY DISCUSSION: A TROUBLESHOOTING GUIDE

The following section examines some challenges of leading discussion and suggests ways in which you can address them. For in-depth instructions on conducting Shared Inquiry Discussion, see chapter 3.*

For the Read-Aloud program, see Sharing Questions Discussion: A Variant for Read-Aloud Participants, pp. 92–93.

When difficulties arise in discussion, as they do for even the most experienced leaders, continue to work within the framework of the rules of Shared Inquiry Discussion. By dealing with problems within the context of your role as leader, you will encourage the best creative and cooperative efforts of your group. Moreover, you will minimize inhibitions caused by the fear of failure and help make discussion a freer, more comfortable exchange of ideas.

COMMENTS NOT FOCUSED ON TEXT

When participants' comments stray from the text—for example, students answer questions about a story by talking about themselves and their own experiences—ask a follow-up question that returns their attention to the text:

Leader: Darryl, why does Scho choose a "dangerous seat" when he climbs into the tree?

Darryl: It's dangerous to climb too high up in a tree. When I climb high up in a tree, I get scared.

Leader: Well, do you think Scho knows he is in danger high up in the tree?

Darryl: I don't think so, because it says he "jounced" up and down. He wouldn't do that if he was afraid.

RESPONSES SEEM IRRELEVANT

When a student seems to digress, it may actually reflect a leap of mind into new territory. If you're not sure of the relevance of a response, ask the participant to furnish the connection. Asking participants to explain how their responses relate to the original question will prevent you from overlooking worthwhile ideas.

PARTICIPANTS HAVE NO ANSWERS

A student who has no answer may need more time. After a pause, if you continue to get no response, think of a passage that might clarify the problem and ask the participant to read it aloud and then repeat your question. Try to stay with that student as long as you feel you are accomplishing something in striving for an answer. To give the student more time, ask other participants to help out. You may want to preface your call for additional opinions by saying something such as, "Can anyone help us with this?" or "Does anyone have any ideas?" Ask the student who is having difficulty to listen to the answers other students give. Return to this student before discussion ends to ask if he or she has heard any ideas that helped answer the question.

MISREADINGS OR RECALL PROBLEMS

If participants forget important details or offer interpretations based on a misreading of the text, use follow-up questions to help them recall the facts. Ask your participants to read and closely examine a relevant passage. This is also a good strategy when participants cannot locate the facts they need to support a reasonable opinion. Make sure your participants keep their books open throughout discussion. Encourage them to refer to the text often to look for examples and check ideas.

VOCABULARY PROBLEMS

If participants have difficulty understanding a particular word or phrase in a selection—and its meaning is important to the matter under discussion—use a synonym or gloss the word in a follow-up question. You can also show students how to search the text for clues to a word's meaning by asking them questions that guide them to do so. First, ask for a rough definition, then in follow-up questions inquire about the word's connections in context. Guide participants to relate what is said about the word to the interpretive issues in the selection. In this way, they will see how the meaning of the word both derives from and contributes to the context in which it is used. If your group requires a more formal definition, ask someone to look the word up, but continue discussion until a dictionary definition can be introduced. Then ask participants to relate the dictionary meaning of the word to how it is used in the selection.

SHY PARTICIPANTS

Participants who are initially shy and hesitant about expressing their ideas, or who tend merely to agree with their friends, can be drawn out if you show that their insights are useful to the group. Return to the ideas that they do express, and ask others in the group to consider them: "Antonio, do you agree with Sarah's idea that . . . ?" Be persistent in directing questions to them by name and listening carefully to what they say.*

See also Questions from the Field, p. 76.

OVERLY TALKATIVE PARTICIPANTS

Participants who dominate discussion can create problems by intimidating shy or less-articulate participants into complete silence. You can check this in a positive, productive way by asking someone else to evaluate or comment on one of the ideas offered by the too-talkative participant: "Alex, can you wait just a minute? Monique, do you agree with what Alex just said, that . . . ?" This strategy gets everyone's attention. It also selects a portion of the response to pursue, slows the rush of ideas, and involves other participants. You can also ask those more vocal participants to respond to ideas they have not originated, thus encouraging them to listen more patiently to others in the group.

UNINTERESTED OR CONFUSED PARTICIPANTS

If students seem uninterested in or confused by your basic question, try rephrasing it:

Dialogue

Leader: Why does Scho enlarge the scope of his game
at the end of the story?

Shawn: I don't know.

Leader: At the end of the story, why does Scho say,
"I want you to do whatever you're going to do for
the whole rest of your life"?

Sometimes, when you rephrase your question, it may be helpful to give a participant a choice of alternatives that reflect your curiosity about an answer:

Leader: Why does Scho climb the tree when Glennie and
   Monk do not let him play?

Jordan: I don't know.

Leader: Do you think Scho was angry when he climbed
   the tree, or maybe embarrassed?

Jordan: I think he might have felt embarrassed because
   he got left out. And so he climbed the tree to get
   their attention and show off.

You might also ask students to read aloud a passage that originally suggested the question to you. This may help them to see what the problem of meaning is. Or, use another question from your cluster to help your participants begin to answer your basic question. If the group seems to be having trouble with the subject matter of the basic question, ask questions to find out exactly what the difficulty is.

WRITING

Although most of the Junior Great Books interpretive activities can be conducted orally, we strongly recommend that you also use the companion writing activities. By allowing students to keep track of their reactions and see how their

Questions from the Field

How can I handle student complaints that the story is "boring" or "dumb"?

Most students enjoy the stories. But if some participants dislike a selection, often it's because they had trouble reading it. Perhaps its style is challenging, its vocabulary unfamiliar, or the experience it presents seems remote. In such cases, you need to allow time for your group to grasp the facts of the story before conducting Shared Inquiry Discussion. In addition to the interpretive activities suggested for the unit, you may find it helpful to take some time to review the facts of the story with students. Help participants see the structure of the work by asking questions that draw their attention to connections between passages. If students complain that a selection is too long, you may want to break it into smaller sections, dividing it at natural breaking points in the story.

Conducting textual analysis on a key passage can highlight important themes or ideas while focusing on a portion of text that is more manageable for students. Direct your participants to a passage and ask questions to take them through it carefully. If you are doing this during Shared Inquiry Discussion, pay particular attention to ideas and details related to your basic question.

To deal with criticism of a selection that arises during Shared Inquiry Discussion,

proceed as you normally would, but encourage your participants to raise objections whenever they become relevant in discussion. If complaints are so strong that they prevent your group from beginning to answer your basic question, address them more directly. For example, if your participants think a selection is "boring," ask them where it was most boring and what makes it boring. Is it the writer's style or the characters and plot? Press your participants to be specific. If the story is "not realistic," find out where your participants think it is most unrealistic and ask them to explain their judgment. What would have to be changed to make it "real"? Why does the author do it this way? If your participants dislike a character or feel a character is not credible, ask why. In the same situation, how would they act differently? What is it about the character that makes him or her behave this way?

What does the author gain by having such a character?

Your purpose in asking these questions is not to defend the selection but to get your participants thinking about the text. Many times, complaints will disappear as your group gets more involved with a work. In the process of explaining and supporting their complaints with specific evidence, participants may even uncover new interpretive issues. Thus, the comment "It's stupid for Scho to climb up the tree so far" can lead to *Why does Scho climb up so high?* As soon as your follow-up questions uncover a possibly fruitful and relevant interpretive problem, pursue it. Then return to your original question.

Your participants do not have to like a selection to have a good discussion of it. In fact, one of the objectives of Junior Great Books is to help students move from tentative first impressions of a work—whether positive or negative—to sounder judgments of what the work means. By making negative responses a useful part of discussion and showing that you respect well-founded complaints, you will help your participants become more discerning readers— more willing to get past their initial reactions and consider each work on its own terms.

thinking changes over the course of working on a unit, writing helps students extend the process of reflection and the search for meaning in literature. To help students learn to improve their writing, guide them in developing their first drafts into more finished products by asking the kinds of follow-up questions you use in discussion.

CAPTIONS AND GROUP WRITING
(GRADES K-1)

When students write captions for pictures, ask them to relate the caption to elements in the drawing. In this way students begin to grasp the relevance of a piece of writing. They also begin to get a rudimentary idea of evidence—how the elements in the picture support the caption.

During group creative writing, be sure to model the entire writing process by letting students share in a prewriting brainstorming session. Ask questions that prompt students to think about what should be included in the piece of writing and what should be left out. Once a piece seems complete, ask if it needs any changes to make it sound better. Allow students to enjoy their finished product by having them read it aloud as a group or letting them copy it onto their own papers.

CREATIVE WRITING AND PERSONAL AND EVALUATIVE ESSAYS (GRADES 2-6)

When commenting on students' prediscussion written work, keep in mind that its chief purpose is to help students try out interpretive ideas and gradually clarify them. It is work in progress. Better responses are those that show thoughtfulness, clarity, and a willingness to give reasons and evidence from the text.

POSTDISCUSSION WRITING OPTIONS

Although some units contain two or more postdiscussion writing activities, students are not expected to complete all of the options. Make sure students understand that they can choose the writing assignment that provides the best avenue for extending their thinking about the selection.

RESPONDING TO WRITING

When commenting on a student's written work, focus on how directly and thoughtfully it responds to the assignment and how well ideas are supported. Ask yourself:

- Are the ideas clearly stated?

- Are the supporting details or evidence relevant to what the student is trying to say?

- Is the assignment complete?

At the middle and high school levels, you will want to see that students can handle more complexity in their writing. Ask yourself:

- Does the essay or story cover the whole topic, or respond to only part of it?

- Is the essay or story coherent?

- Are ideas and opinions supported with reasons, evidence, examples, and details? Are these presented accurately and fully so that their logical connection is clear?

- Does the essay weigh ideas and consider different sides of a issue?

In your comments, point out the parts of the work that meet these criteria, so that students can recognize and build on their accomplishments.

In addition, correct errors in grammar, spelling, and punctuation in later drafts, especially if the pieces will be published. Making your district's or state's writing rubric available to students as they plan and revise can also help them understand the qualities of good writing.

The postdiscussion writing activity pages can be used as a short-answer writing assignment or as the basis for planning a more extended piece of written work, such as a story, poem, personal essay, or evaluative essay. Explain to students that thinking about each of the guiding questions on their activity pages will help them get ideas and organize their writing. You might have a few volunteers share with the rest of the class their initial thoughts about how they will respond in their essays.

If you intend for students to use the activity page as the basis of an extended writing assignment, make sure they understand that they should make notes on the activity page and can work with the guiding questions in whatever order they find most helpful. In some cases, it may be easier for them to formulate the main idea or topic sentence last, after the guiding questions on the activity page have been answered. After answering the guiding questions, students will be ready to think about how they want to organize their notes into a finished essay or story. With your help, students might number the guiding questions to indicate the order in which they want to address them in their final drafts. Give older students time to plan, revise, and create final drafts of the postdiscussion writing activities they choose. You should consult your Teacher's Edition for grade-appropriate suggestions for conducting the writing activities that are specific to your series.

Occasionally, you might need students to explain their thinking behind a beginning piece of writing. Meet briefly with each student while the class works or as they hand in their papers. You can help them articulate their ideas by asking about what you do not understand. Remember that answers that seem odd or incomplete on paper are first steps and, with clarification, may represent good insights.

WRITING AFTER DISCUSSION (GRADES 7–12)

Your Leader's Guide suggests postdiscussion writing topics that you or your students can choose from. To help students come up with ideas for their writing, conduct a prewriting brainstorming session in which you help them generate a short list of guiding questions. These questions can help students through the composition process by prompting them to elaborate on their ideas. As students plan their writing, draw their attention to guiding questions they have overlooked. When appropriate, have students do their prewriting work in pairs or small groups.

After you have helped students generate a list of guiding questions, you might want to have a few volunteers share some initial thoughts. Encourage students who have difficulty putting their thoughts on paper to talk through their ideas before writing; have students discuss the guiding questions in small groups or pairs before writing. Once students have generated a number of ideas, they may want to create an outline to help them order their ideas.

Chapter Highlight

Dramatization and Junior Great Books

Dramatization is an excellent way to enrich discussion of a selection and can be readily adapted for many different types of groups and circumstances. Even older and more sophisticated students will welcome the opportunity to engage with literature in this immediate, creative way.

> Many suggestions for dramatizations are given in the Teacher's Editions for the Read-Aloud program and Junior Great Books Series 2, but if you are working with another series, the following criteria will help you select passages suitable for dramatization.
>
> 1. Consider the scene's inherent dramatic potential.
>
>   Is it fairly self-contained?
>
>   Does it emphasize character confrontation or conflict?
>
>   Is there good dialogue?
>
> 2. Look for passages or scenes that have interpretive richness to support the extra attention.
>
> 3. Choose scenes that are particularly funny. Such scenes are usually great favorites for both the actors and the audience.

Before discussion. Dramatizations conducted before Shared Inquiry Discussion can help students empathize with the characters in a story and experiment with various insights. Textual analysis is also a good place to introduce dramatization. It is especially effective if you want students to focus on a particularly dense or subtle passage. Students will get more from acting out a scene if they first have a chance to look closely at the passage and work with its unusual language. Before the dramatization, spend a few moments discussing the scene, asking students to consider various interpretations.

After discussion. Dramatizations used after Shared Inquiry Discussion give students the opportunity to consolidate their work on the selection and to think further about the various ideas expressed by their classmates. Young participants especially appreciate the closure provided by a relatively simple activity, such as miming the action of a significant final scene as you read it aloud or chorusing distinctive phrases or passages in the selection. More experienced students can work in small groups, with each group preparing one key scene from the story to be presented in a concluding, informal dramatization of the whole selection.

With writing. You can use dramatization as an occasional alternative, or complement, to writing. For instance, students might write scripts based on the selection and then perform their "play" for the group. In addition to gaining experience in writing dialogue, participants can utilize their new, deepened understanding of the story and its characters.

At the end of a unit. For a culminating activity on a unit, older students may enjoy presenting and comparing back-to-back dramatizations of the same scene with different casts, or being involved in directing or critiquing a performance. This is an especially good way to increase small-group work in your program. Your class can split up into teams to develop different scenes or different interpretations of the same action. If you are doing a whole-class dramatization of a selection, consider sharing the key role, or roles, among several different people. Not only do more students have a chance to play a lead part, but the whole group also has an opportunity to observe different interpretations.

With ample time and an ambitious group, you might consider mounting a full-scale production. Works like our selection from *Alice's Adventures in Wonderland* (Series 4, First Semester) and *The Strange Case of Dr. Jekyll and Mr. Hyde* (Series 9) are inherently dramatic and afford plenty of opportunities for everyone to be involved. In addition to acting in the final production, participants can all work together or split into smaller groups to develop a script, direct, research costumes and sets, select background music, and design special effects. Even putting together a modest production of such stories can give children a fresh sense of the excitement of literature and enhance the atmosphere of cooperative learning.

✳ ✳ ✳

However you decide to incorporate dramatization into your Junior Great Books program, try to ensure that all members of your group who wish to participate have a chance to do so. Dramatization not only helps students better comprehend and extend their thinking about the selection—it's fun! Regardless of their acting ability, students enjoy bringing a story to life by acting it out. And by doing so, they learn to experience and appreciate literature in a new way.

Chapter Review

1. Your training as a leader of Shared Inquiry Discussion will prepare you to lead the other Junior Great Books interpretive activities, but the model you present to students—someone intellectually engaged with literature—is the most important teaching strategy in the Shared Inquiry approach to learning.

2. Each activity is distinct in purpose and rhythm. Keep the objective of each activity in mind as you conduct it, remembering that the goal is not to exhaust the topic but to help students overcome obstacles to understanding and to give them opportunities to develop and build on ideas as work on the unit progresses.

3. To prepare to conduct the activities, begin as you would for Shared Inquiry Discussion—read the selection twice, take notes, and identify the interpretive issues by writing questions. As an additional part of your preparation, you may find it helpful to do some of the activities, particularly the note-taking suggestions.

4. Although the other interpretive activities are not intended to replicate Shared Inquiry Discussion, you should maintain an atmosphere of Shared Inquiry as you conduct each activity by asking questions that prompt thoughtful inquiry, by encouraging students to share a variety of responses, and by asking students to provide examples, reasons, or other support for their ideas when appropriate.

Chapter 5

IMPLEMENTING

JUNIOR GREAT BOOKS

Junior Great Books is for all students, but not all Junior Great Books programs are implemented in the same way. In many areas of the country, Junior Great Books has traditionally been known as a once-a-week, literature-based, enrichment program led by parent volunteers. In a growing number of schools, Junior Great Books is used as a daily program that helps fulfill the core reading and language arts objectives of critical thinking, reading comprehension, oral communication, and writing. In addition, Junior Great Books has always enjoyed a reputation as an excellent program for gifted and talented students.

Whatever goals you set for your program, Junior Great Books provides all students with the opportunity for intellectual growth through the use of quality literature. It inspires students to raise questions and search for answers, share ideas and work with their classmates as partners in learning, and experience the exhilaration of taking on a challenge.

Junior Great Books reaches students on many levels—the more time you give the program, the greater the impact on student learning.

CUSTOMIZING YOUR JUNIOR GREAT BOOKS PROGRAM

Your implementation will depend on your goals for the program and the student outcomes you wish to achieve. When planning your implementation, keep in mind that Junior Great Books is primarily a program about ideas—understanding ideas presented in literature, sharing ideas with others, and learning from the ideas of others. It is about improving one's own thinking by articulating, clarifying, and supporting positions in discussion and in writing. Through participating in the literary experience of reading and discussion, students increase their capacity to understand complex ideas as presented in a work of literature and develop their ability to effectively communicate with others. Proficiency in comprehension and communication comes not from practicing discrete skills in isolation but from using these skills in combination. Most schools find that in order to give students adequate practice and support in this type of work, they need to schedule Junior Great Books activities three to four days per week and need to complete at least one semester of materials.

Some schools train their entire staff in the Shared Inquiry method. Others build effective programs through the collaborative efforts of teachers, parents, and members of the community. But all of these Junior Great Books implementations have one thing in common—under the guidance of trained leaders, students participate in Shared Inquiry Discussion of the selections published by the Great Books Foundation.

In-School, Whole-Class Programs

Junior Great Books invites collaboration between teachers and volunteers. If yours is an in-school, whole-class program, trained volunteers can lead half the class in Shared Inquiry Discussion while the teacher leads the other half. This will make discussion more intimate and productive, with each student having more chances to participate. Volunteers can also help lead other interpretive activities.

Volunteer-Led, Once-a-Week Programs

If your program is a volunteer-led, once-a-week program, volunteers may want to assign the Directed Notes activity as homework for the following week's selection. Another possibility is to introduce the story and read it aloud one week and discuss it the next. Volunteers are also encouraged to be open to students' questions, perhaps giving students time to voice their curiosity before discussion starts. Although volunteer leaders are encouraged to use the Teacher's Edition or Leader's Guide to help them with their preparation and leading, we do not recommend that volunteer-led, once-a-week programs try to replicate in-class programs by conducting many of the activities beyond two readings and note taking.

Once-a-Week, Pullout Programs

If yours is a once-a-week, pullout program, you can enrich your discussions by using the interpretive activities. The activities reinforce the Junior Great Books model of active reading—reading twice, taking notes, and formulating interpretive questions—that leaders have always encouraged students to follow. Ask the students' regular classroom teacher to do the first reading in class. (All students will enjoy hearing the stories read aloud, whether or not they participate in the program.) To encourage students to complete a thoughtful second reading of a selection, assign the Directed Notes activity when you assign each story, then begin your meetings with a brief sharing of notes. To emphasize the connection between writing and thinking, ask the classroom teacher to assign some of the activity pages—especially the creative writing and essays—as independent language arts work or as homework. These simple additions will build a firmer commitment to your program and will make your discussion more lively and focused. You might also expand the program to meet twice a week so that you can lead some of the interpretive activities yourself.

WORKING WITH SPECIAL POPULATIONS

Junior Great Books has been the subject of academic research and evaluation by a number of educational organizations. Junior Great Books has been specifically recognized for its effectiveness with gifted students and middle school students and has been used successfully with Title I students, young children, ESL students, and students in heterogeneous classrooms. Lower-ability readers who participate in Junior Great Books show gains in reading comprehension as well as in their ability to answer both factual and interpretive questions.

Read-Aloud Note

IMPLEMENTATION GUIDELINES

The Read-Aloud program should not be implemented as a once-a-week or pull-out program. Kindergarten and first-grade students cannot prepare for interpretive discussion on their own, as older children can. To arrive at thoughtful interpretations, young children need the structure of the repeated readings as well as the interpretive activities, which are designed to build on each other and provide prereaders with concrete help in exploring literature. Through interpretive art activities, dramatizations, group composition, and above all, sharing ideas aloud, young students can begin to internalize the process of thoughtful reading that they will practice in the Junior Great Books program for upper grades.

Of course, parents play a vital role in the Read-Aloud program when they read aloud and discuss G.B.'s questions with their children and help them write down their favorite questions and new vocabulary words. And trained volunteers can still help in the classroom by leading Sharing Questions Discussion and any of the other Read-Aloud activities.

Part of the reason Junior Great Books benefits all students is the program's consistent focus on open-ended, interpretive questions. When students are given genuine problems of meaning to which they can all respond, their own ideas and curiosity impel them to think for themselves. For the latest information on research and a list of organizations that have recognized the effective-ness of Junior Great Books with special popu-lations, please write or call us at the Great Books Foundation.

Questions from the Field

I remember Junior Great Books from when I was in school. Isn't it a program that parents conduct?

Since 1962, parents have shared their love of reading with children by organizing Junior Great Books programs in their schools and becoming discussion leaders themselves. These programs have provided an important opportunity for students to meet and talk about challenging literature. Some students have entered a once-a-week program on a parent's request even though they weren't particularly strong or avid readers. In many cases, these students emerged as enthusiastic readers who as adults, in turn, volunteered to lead groups of young readers.

As schools have become aware of the numerous student benefits to be gained from a Junior Great Books implementation, the use of Junior Great Books as an in-school, whole-class program has been growing steadily. A significant number of Junior Great Books programs around the country are still led by parent volunteers, but today there are many other ways parents can contribute to the program. They can support the program by learning about it, letting teachers know that they endorse it, and raising funds to support it. As at-home partners, parents are an important resource for school-based Junior Great Books implementations, helping students with extra readings and taking students' questions. Parents can also work with teachers to allow for the smaller groups that facilitate the exchange of ideas. Parents who wish to assist in this way must attend our Basic Leader Training Course.

GIFTED STUDENTS

Gifted students thrive when exposed to the rich literature and stimulating intellectual environment created by a Junior Great Books implementation. The reading and discussion format encourages students to be conceptual in their thinking and to pursue patterns, connections, and major themes that appear in literature. The focus on interpretation and emphasis on the use of evidence means that students with diverse opinions can share and explore their ideas in depth. The literature contained in Junior Great Books anthologies has sufficient depth, complexity, and challenge for students to use the series corresponding to their grade level—you need not move up a series. Below are some suggestions for tailoring your program to gifted students.

Allow ample time for Shared Inquiry Discussion. Discussion provides the perfect venue for gifted students to take risks and think divergently. Allow enough time for students to explore their various ideas in depth and examine and compare evidence supporting differing interpretations.

Conduct several of the unit's activities during class time. Conducting several of the unit's activities gives students the opportunity to work with an idea over a period of days and to examine it from various perspectives.

Allow for various modes of interpretive expression. In addition to the opportunities for speaking and writing, you may want to include options for drawing or dramatizing scenes from the story. (These options are already included in the Read-Aloud program and Junior Great Books Series 2.) If your students are interested in dramatic interpretation, you may want to consider staging a full-scale production of a selection as a culminating activity on a unit.

Keep questions and activities open-ended. Using open-ended versions of interpretive questions allows students the most flexibility in answering questions. Treating the activities as open-ended lets students set their own limits and allows them to go as far as they can in developing their thinking.

MIDDLE SCHOOL STUDENTS

Students in the middle grades are often trying to make sense of themselves and the world around them. Although they want to think and act more independently than they did in elementary school, they still need the security of rules and want the respect of their peers. The discipline provided by the four rules of Shared Inquiry Discussion ensures that discussion is both intellectually rigorous and respectful. Students are free to form their own opinions but are expected to support those opinions with evidence from the text.

> Vary activities to allow for individual, small-group, and whole-class work.

The Junior Great Books anthologies for the middle grades contain culturally diverse literature that expresses universal themes. While reading and discussing the selections, students can both explore the larger world and reflect on issues such as interpersonal relationships, the transition from childhood to adulthood, and facing difficult decisions. The following suggestions can help you customize your program for middle school students.

Allow time for small-group work. Students have more autonomy when contributing to small-group projects but still receive the support of their classmates.

Make sure everyone contributes during discussion. Draw out reticent participants to show students that you value everyone's insights. Make sure that students who have unusual answers have time to explain and support their ideas. In order to encourage students to behave properly during discussion, you may want to lead them in verbally assessing the group's performance: Did everyone come prepared? Were answers clearly stated? Did participants offer evidence to support answers? Were opinions respected?

Allow time for students to ask and answer their own questions. Students learn to use their own curiosity about the story as a tool for learning.

Allow students to express their interpretations in various ways. Although Junior Great Books for the middle grades provides ample writing and speaking opportunities, you may want to consider students' other strengths, such as dramatic reading or artistic ability, when working with a selection.

Extend work on a selection into other areas of your curriculum. Because of their multicultural nature, many of the selections in the middle grades can be used in joint language arts/social studies or language arts/history projects.

Incorporate your local writing rubric into the writing component. The ability to state a main idea clearly and support it is important both in Shared Inquiry Discussion and in good expository writing. Using your state's or district's writing rubric during the writing activities will help students learn the qualities of good writing while they learn to use writing as a means of better understanding the selection.

At-Risk, ESL, Title I, and Other Readers Needing Extra Support

There is no better way to involve less-proficient readers in the higher-level thinking that occurs in Junior Great Books than to implement the full range of Junior Great Books interpretive activities. The activities were designed for use in a heterogeneous classroom that includes less-able readers. The focus on interpretation makes it possible for each student to start working from his or her own level of ability. The range of interpretive activities in Junior Great Books allows students with different learning styles to work from their strengths, while gaining practice in areas of weaker skills.

The following suggestions, which draw on the activities, will help you involve below-grade-level readers. Since the Junior Great Books anthologies are recommended for grade-level readers and above, you may want to drop down a series if you have a large number of students who are reading below grade level. However, because stories are also selected for their age appeal, we generally do not recommend dropping down more than two series, regardless of students' reading level.

Conduct all the activities orally. Hearing the stories read aloud and sharing thoughts without first having to write them down can help students, especially young children and ESL students, focus on the ideas without struggling with the decoding and writing skills they have not yet mastered. During Junior Great Books, students will not develop the ability to get a sense of the work as a whole, to make connections with the text and with other students' ideas, and to weigh evidence and think about their reasons for their answers if they are preoccupied with identifying or trying to find the correct spelling for each word.

Give students a chance to hear the story read aloud several times. When students grasp the story as a whole, they will work more confidently on both decoding and comprehension. You might read the story aloud in class two or even three times, or you might create a "listening corner" utilizing the audiotapes available for the Read-Aloud program and Junior Great Books Series 2–6. If students participate in pullout enrichment classes, ask their teachers to use Junior Great Books activities for some of their work. Students can also help each other read by working in pairs or small groups and prompting each other when needed. In some schools, older students serve as reading tutors to help beginners.

Make time for students to ask questions. Setting aside a few minutes after the first reading of a story for students to ask questions and share their reactions provides you with the opportunity to resolve some of their difficulties. Give students time to put their questions into words. If they look puzzled, ask them if they would like to hear part of the story again. If students are able, have them write their questions, in order to help them set an agenda for active reading. Check written questions immediately so that you can address factual questions early on. Another possibility is to arrange students' questions in groups on a Junior Great Books bulletin board,

See Classroom Management Tip, p. 108.

so students get a sense of the issues their classmates see in the story.

Add dramatizations or interpretive art activities to your students' preparation. Choose a dramatic moment from a story for students to act out or illustrate, and lead short discussions that bring out students' different interpretations. You can enhance the interpretive value of a simple dramatization by linking it to students' work on the interpretive activities. For example, if your group does round-robin reading, encourage students to use their vocal tone to convey their interpretations of the story's tone and how it affects meaning and expresses character. You might want to couple these activities with a brief textual analysis.

For younger students, a whole-class improvisation based on the main events of the story can serve as an enjoyable substitute for a plot review before discussion. Recitation or choral reading is fun and suitable for students of all ages as a way of helping them appreciate unique features of style or language.

Keep the focus on interpretation. Interpretive questions are actually easier to start answering than factual ones because each student can draw on whatever part of the story he or she recalls best, rather than having to remember the specific detail a factual question intends to elicit. Answering interpretive questions helps readers see details in a story as important and interesting, because they contribute to the meaning of the whole.

Maintain high expectations for Shared Inquiry Discussion and do not assume that your students are "not ready" for such a high-level activity. Lead a small group, giving each student many chances to speak. Show sincere interest in participants' ideas by encouraging them to explain and give reasons for their answers. Help out by directing them to passages that might provide evidence.

Involve students' parents. Be sure the parents of your less-proficient readers understand how much their children have to gain from Junior Great Books, and that reading with their children can ensure full involvement in the program. Students will work more confidently and progress more rapidly on both decoding and comprehension the more they are read to at home. However, if parents are unable to assist with at-home readings, reading buddies and the Junior Great Books audiotapes for the Read-Aloud program and Series 2–6 can also help enrich students' oral language experience.

Lead the activities patiently. Ask students to explain and support their responses and to comment on each other's ideas. Let them see that you have serious expectations for their oral work. Involve the whole class; keep a seating chart or a class list on which to check off names so you can keep track of individual contributions. Stress collaborative work.

Divide the class into small groups. In small groups, students have more chances to speak and hear others respond to their ideas. Try some of the suggestions for small-group work in your Teacher's Edition as a way to give everyone more opportunities to participate in the activities.*

See also Dividing Your Class for Discussion, pp. 94–95.

Provide extra help with vocabulary. The selections in Junior Great Books present challenging vocabulary for students. Rather than reinforcing students' insecurity about what they do not know, present vocabulary as an opportunity for discovery. Have students keep lists of words they find interesting and unusual. This practice can enhance their pleasure in the language of a story and also increase their sight vocabularies. They can keep these lists in a Junior Great Books notebook. After they have made several lists, they may enjoy creating their own dictionaries or glossaries.*

See also Working with Challenging Vocabulary, pp. 114–116.

Provide extra support for writing. Use a brainstorming or other prewriting session to help beginning writers get their ideas down on paper, and be available to help students who get stuck. Ask questions to help them talk through what they want to say before writing it. Encourage invented spelling on first drafts. Or, write on the board proper names and words from the story that students might need. Having the class suggest words for this list can help them start thinking about what they will write. If you are publishing the class's work, students may want to help each other correct grammar and spelling, or you can correct it yourself.

After the class completes oral work, such as discussing the Directed Notes or Interpreting Words activities, students should be prepared to answer the session's closing question in writing. This activity can also be conducted orally. Ask the group to contribute several answers, and write them on the board. Then have students copy the answer of their choice.

The postdiscussion writing activities can also be conducted orally. Children who wish to complete them independently can do so while you lead a small group through the full process of writing an essay, story, or poem. First, have the group suggest what thoughts or ideas they would like to include. Then let them compose a draft, which you write on the board or on chart paper. Finally, read their draft back to them so they can make revisions. Whenever possible, have students copy down their completed work, not only so they can practice their writing, but also so they can include the finished product in their Junior Great Books notebooks.

Dictating also helps beginners learn to compose longer pieces and gain confidence. They might dictate to you, to a more skillful student, or to parents or siblings at home. To take dictation, place the paper where the student can watch you write, and sound out the words as you form them. Take down exactly what the student says; corrections can come later. If the student loses focus or reaches an impasse, help out with questions based on what he or she has already written.

Chapter Highlight

Implementation Guidelines for Principals

We want your Junior Great Books program to succeed. Experience has shown us that the most successful and effective programs are the ones in which teachers, principals, and other administrators share an understanding of Junior Great Books.

REFER TO THE FOLLOWING CHECKLIST AS YOU PLAN YOUR IMPLEMENTATION:

- ❑ Plan to use Junior Great Books regularly, consistently, and across the grades.
- ❑ Give your staff the resources they need: training, materials, and follow-up support.
- ❑ Schedule regular time in the school day for program use. We recommend at least three sessions per week.
- ❑ Allow sufficient time for teachers to become accomplished in Shared Inquiry. It takes time and practice to become skillful at inquiry-based instruction.
- ❑ Appoint someone to coordinate the Junior Great Books program at your school.

CONSIDER THE FOLLOWING STEPS AS YOU PLAN:

1. Identify which curricular, academic, or students' needs you will meet with Junior Great Books.

2. Determine how the program will fit into your school's schedule.

3. Work with your staff to develop a shared understanding of

   - Why you are implementing Junior Great Books

   - Where Junior Great Books will fit into your curriculum (including what it will complement or displace in the existing curriculum)

   - How much time you expect teachers to devote to Junior Great Books

4. Determine how and when you will assess the program's impact on student learning.

5. Decide whether you will budget for a team, schoolwide, or larger-scale implementation, and establish your source of funding.

6. Hold a pretraining orientation meeting with teachers to clarify the plan, explain how Junior Great Books will meet students' needs, work out the practical details of implementing the program, and get them excited about adopting a new approach to teaching.

KEEP THE FOLLOWING RECOMMENDATIONS IN MIND:

■ Schedule training so that everyone involved with program use at your school can attend the same course and support each other as they learn.

■ Purchase Junior Great Books materials when you schedule training so that teachers can begin using the program immediately after completing the course.

■ Take advantage of the Foundation's other training and consultation offerings. Our program coordinator for your area can advise you on which materials and offerings will best support your Junior Great Books implementation.

As you go forward with your implementation, remember that the Basic Leader Training Course must be completed by all Junior Great Books leaders and anyone else who will conduct or support your program (principals and other administrators, support teachers, paraprofessionals, volunteers).

Chapter Review

1. Although Junior Great Books has a long history as a parent volunteer program and has an excellent reputation for use with gifted students, more schools today integrate Junior Great Books into their language arts curriculum for the typical, mixed-ability classroom.

2. With the exception of the Read-Aloud program, you need not conduct all of the activities in class. At-home activities for the Read-Aloud program are clearly identified.

3. Although a variety of implementations exist—from once-a-week, extracurricular programs to daily, whole-class programs—most schools find that three to four days a week is necessary to give students time to read the selection twice, take notes, share questions, work with important vocabulary, and participate in Shared Inquiry Discussion.

4. Since the activities are interpretive, and in many cases open-ended, students of varying abilities can benefit from participating in them. The nature of the activities also allows you to adapt the activities to better meet the needs of particular students.

5. Regardless of the type of implementation you choose, for all age and ability levels, students should be given opportunities to raise questions about the selections and to share their ideas.

6. When planning a Junior Great Books implementation, make sure that all leaders will receive training and that all students will have access to materials.

Chapter 6

BEGINNING YOUR

JUNIOR GREAT BOOKS

PROGRAM

In the Basic Leader Training Course, you learned how to identify problems of interpretation, how to formulate questions specific to a selection, and how to guide students in reading and reflecting on stories. You practiced preparing for and leading Shared Inquiry Discussion. Now you are ready to begin.

Leading Shared Inquiry Discussion holds many rewards, but the spontaneity and independent thinking that make Shared Inquiry so exciting can present some difficulties for beginning leaders as well as participants. One former course participant wrote us:

> When I completed my Junior Great Books training course,
> I was confident that I could lead, but wondered if my
> students were ready for Shared Inquiry. After my first couple
> of discussions, I wasn't sure any of us were ready. By the
> end of the first year, we were all having a great time—and
> I had redefined "ready"!

This type of experience is not uncommon. Children do not come to a work of literature or to discussion with the same aptitudes or attitudes as adults. For many, interpretive reading and thinking is new and demanding. Most leaders need time and practice to feel confident in their ability to identify the interpretive questions that make discussion "take off" and to respond to students with effective follow-up questions.

INTRODUCING YOUR STUDENTS TO SHARED INQUIRY

As you introduce your students to interpretive reading and discussion, here are some things to keep in mind.

1. *Encourage reflection.* Your students may not be accustomed to taking the time to explore and master difficult language and ideas. As a Junior Great Books leader, you model reflective thinking for your students. Share your curiosity with them. Explain how something in the text became a question for you. You can give students time to share questions in class, post their questions on a Junior Great Books bulletin board, or use their questions in Shared Inquiry Discussion.

2. *Give students time to think.* Appreciate and encourage the small, silent moments when children wrestle with understanding and communicating. Try not to feel uncomfortable if your group is quiet for a time. Quiet consideration of a passage in the story or of another student's idea is often necessary for a student to arrive at just what he or she wants to say. If during discussion a student needs more time to form his or her response, note on your seating chart the need to return to that student. Remember, you are after quality and depth of response—not quantity and speed of answers.

Why does Shared Inquiry focus just on interpretive questions? Shouldn't I also ask students factual or evaluative questions?

Questions from the Field

In Shared Inquiry, we focus on interpretive questions because they promote reflection about the deeper meaning of literature. Factual questions—questions about the selection that have only one correct answer—have limited use in Shared Inquiry. Because the answer to a factual question establishes a fact of the story, you may want to ask a factual question to clarify an assertion, bring out a piece of evidence, focus students' attention on a particular passage, or test an answer.

By participating in the unit's interpretive activities, students usually attain an adequate grasp of the facts of a story prior to discussion. Remember, it isn't necessary for students to master all the facts of the story in order to begin the process of interpretation.

Sometimes, though, students fail to understand the facts of the story, even after a careful reading, because they lack contextual information—historical or cultural references that students don't understand. When dealing with these situations, allow students to raise the questions themselves during Sharing Questions or while sharing notes. Since the goal of Shared Inquiry is to instill the habits of self-reliant thinking, reading, and learning, students should try answering their own questions

rather than look to you to supply the missing information. (If you make a habit of providing the answers, students will come to expect this assistance and will not develop their own abilities to find things out for themselves.) Try to devise a way for students to discover the information for themselves—direct them to the appropriate reference material, ask other students for answers, or let students work together in small groups to piece together information, if possible.

As for evaluative questions, in Shared Inquiry, students are encouraged to focus on the meaning of the text and to defer judgment about the selection as a whole until they have completed their work of interpretation. If evaluative questions are introduced too early in the reading process, they are likely to elicit only personal opinions having little to do with genuine learning. Another danger is that the evaluation itself will be weak

because it lacks a strong interpretive base.

In contrast, asking students for personal reactions toward a character or situation in a story can be an effective way of involving them more deeply in the interpretive process. For example, if students participating in a Shared Inquiry Discussion of Hans Christian Andersen's "The Ugly Duckling" have trouble responding to the question *Why doesn't the duckling get angry at the way the hen and the cat treat him?*, a skilled leader might ask, "How would you feel if the hen told you to keep quiet because you couldn't lay eggs?" After collecting a number of different answers, the leader could then return to the original interpretive question by asking, "Why do you think the duckling doesn't get mad when the hen says this?"

Because they arise from interpretations of the text, evaluative questions are best addressed after you have conducted a careful interpretive discussion of the selection. If students' interpretations of a selection are very diverse, there may be little common ground from which to begin a discussion. Allowing students to pursue their own ideas through writing may be a better approach in this instance.

3. *Ask follow-up questions.* During Shared Inquiry Discussion and the other interpretive activities, ask follow-up questions to help students focus on problems and articulate their responses. At first, students may speak up in discussion, but their contributions may not go beyond retelling parts of the story that they remember or like—whether or not they answer your question. Or, students may be reminded of something that happened to them, and go on to tell a personal story. You will find yourself using a lot more follow-up questions to elicit evidence and to refocus attention on the text. For many students, it is a big step from answering a question to explaining an answer. At first, their simple answers seem obvious to them. If you ask them "Why do you think that?" or "Where in the story did you see that?", they may not know how to respond. But such questions communicate to students your serious interest in what they think. Stay with it and gradually they will catch your curiosity and start thinking further.

HOLDING YOUR FIRST MEETING WITH STUDENTS

Using one of the short readings provided in *Getting Started with Junior Great Books* is an excellent way to initiate your students into Junior Great Books. Conducting the mini-unit with students at your first meeting will allow you to take them through an introduction to the selection, two readings, note taking or G.B.'s questions, a sharing of notes or responses, and a brief Shared Inquiry Discussion. If time permits, you may want to allow students a few minutes to share questions or reactions to the selection after the first reading.

Whether you use a mini-unit or not, you should prepare for your first session as you would for any Junior Great Books selection. Read the selection twice, take notes (including the Directed Notes suggestion on your second reading, for Junior Great Books Series 2–9), write a few interpretive questions, and then select or prepare a basic question and cluster with which to lead Shared Inquiry Discussion. Keep the following steps in mind:

1. Arrange seating in a circle or square to make your classroom more conducive to students sharing ideas.

2. Prepare a seating chart so that you can keep track of students' ideas.

3. Explain to students that the stories they will be reading in Junior Great Books have been selected not only because they are good literature but also because they raise interpretive questions for readers. Give older students a more precise definition of an interpretive question (such as the one provided on page 43). Tell younger students that interpretive questions are fun to talk about and that students do not have to agree with each other about their answers.

4. Emphasize that during Junior Great Books, leaders and participants learn from one another as they share questions and ideas about these selections.

5. If you are using a mini-unit, conduct the activities as listed. If you are using the first selection in a Junior Great Books anthology, conduct the activities listed for session 1 in your Teacher's Edition or Leader's Guide.

CONDUCTING YOUR FIRST SHARED INQUIRY DISCUSSION WITH STUDENTS

Before you begin, explain that discussion will always center on a question that seems important to the group's understanding of the story and for which you do not have an answer. Go over the four rules of Shared Inquiry Discussion (see page 67). Keep the following steps in mind as you lead your students in discussion:

1. State your basic question and give students time to write their answers.

2. Tell your students that they are free to express any opinions or guesses that come to mind in response to your interpretive questions, even if they have not thought the ideas through, but explain that you will be asking for their reasons or evidence for their answers.

3. Encourage your students to listen to the ideas of their fellow students and to ask questions of others when they do not understand something.

KNOWING WHAT TO EXPECT FROM YOUR STUDENTS

Many teachers who are new to Junior Great Books, and particularly to the Read-Aloud program, have asked us to describe the level of participation they should expect from their students. Although students at every grade level will differ, the following guidelines may help you observe the progress your students are making in Junior Great Books.

My students always direct their answers to me during discussion. How can I get them to talk more to each other and get a real discussion going?

Questions from the Field

When you first start a Junior Great Books program, it's natural that students will respond to your questions just as they do in the regular classroom setting. That is, you ask a question and they direct their answers to you. They don't know what a good Shared Inquiry Discussion looks or feels like. Just as you might have to change gears from your usual teaching habits when acting as a Junior Great Books leader, your students have to change gears, too. You can help them become good participants by explaining to them what makes a good discussion, modeling good follow-up skills for them, and encouraging them to interact more.

Before each discussion, remind your students that they are free to add to each other's ideas, to agree and disagree, and even to ask questions of each other. Preface the discussion activity with comments like these: "Vanessa, if you agree or disagree with one of Kyle's ideas, you can just say so. Darius, if Amber says something and you want her to explain further or show you

where she got that idea, just turn to her and ask her your question."

Besides telling students that they are free to interact, you can show them that you want more interaction through your follow-up questions. For example, once a student has given you an answer, ask other participants whether they agree or disagree with that answer. Ask them if they understand the answer or if they see evidence for it: "Does Hannah's answer make sense to you, Ian? Hannah, can you explain to Ian what you were trying to say? Stefan, can you help Hannah find evidence for her idea?" Asking these kinds of questions helps put an individual's answer out on the floor for the whole group to consider.

After your discussion, praise the group for the times that they did interact and let them know that you hope they do more of it the next time. Once students begin to interact and see that it is something you encourage in discussion, they will start working well together as a group. Remember that the other Junior Great Books activities—especially Text Openers, Directed Notes, and Interpreting Words—also provide opportunities for students to discuss specific interpretive issues and become more comfortable with examining ideas as a group.

Sharing their opinions with their peers, considering others' viewpoints, debating issues, and asking lots of their own follow-up questions is what makes Junior Great Books so much fun for students. With that kind of interaction, you can be sure that they have really improved their listening, speaking, and critical-thinking skills.

JUNIOR GREAT BOOKS READ-ALOUD PROGRAM (GRADES K-1)

Kindergarten and first-grade students should not be expected to respond to literature in the same way that older students do. In the Read-Aloud program, students begin to practice interpretive reading skills every time they listen to a story or poem. At first, it may be difficult for them to listen to the stories straight through. As you progress through a series, however, you should begin to see that students are able to listen for longer periods of time. You may find, as well, that students who have trouble listening to a whole story on a first reading can follow along better on a second and third reading as they become more familiar with the selection.

Another way that you can note that students are paying greater attention to what they are hearing is by the questions they ask. Even factual questions suggest that students are paying close attention to the details of the story and are thinking about the selection as you read aloud.

Increasing detail in students' artwork also reflects students' growing thoughtfulness. The artistic quality of the work is not important. What is important is that students are able to explain why they drew the picture the way they did and to refer to the story in describing what their pictures represent.

The content of a student's picture or the caption that a student writes for a picture can also help you to determine if he or she is grasping the concept of relevance—an important skill in higher-order thinking and reasoning. Is the picture appropriate to the assignment? Does the caption go along with the picture?

Although most kindergartners and first graders are limited in their ability to give textual evidence, you can see students making a greater effort to use their reasoning skills as they move from non-answers such as "I don't know" or "Just because" to simple answers such as "That's what I would do."

Keep in mind that the primary purpose of the Read-Aloud program is to give students the sense of what the literary experience of reading is about—to experience rich vocabulary, to work with ideas, to let the written word engage one's imagination—and to use art, drama, discussion, and group writing to express their ideas about the stories and poems.

JUNIOR GREAT BOOKS (GRADES 2–9)

Second grade often marks a transition in intellectual development for students. Like kindergartners and first graders, second graders may have trouble sitting through the oral reading of some of the stories at first. Second graders, however, are usually more verbally responsive during the oral activities. They are better able to recall details from the selection and to support their answers with evidence, although they do not develop their answers in much detail. They need to be prompted to listen to each other. Students in second grade are also able to do more substantive writing, although taking notes is a skill beyond most at this age.

Your students will surprise you with their insights—but take the time to teach them how to give evidence and respond to others' ideas.

By third grade, even students participating in Junior Great Books for the first time are able to be active in the process of interpretive reading and discussion. Students can do at least one of the readings on their own, take Directed Notes, and be interested and productive during Shared Inquiry Discussion. At first, students will not give evidence without being asked, nor will they spontaneously offer clarification of their answers. Through your skillful use of follow-up questions, however, you will begin to see students develop the habit of giving evidence for their answers, clarifying word choices or ideas, and agreeing or disagreeing with others directly.

First-time Shared Inquiry Discussion participants in upper elementary grades and in middle school will quickly pick up the habit of giving evidence, although you will usually need to prompt them to explain how the evidence supports their answers. With your help, these students can stay focused on the story. Students in these grades usually show a greater interest in the responses of others than do younger students, but you may need to facilitate this exchange of ideas by encouraging students to let the speaker have time to explain his or her position before they jump in to disagree. But even in middle school, students' answers often lack depth. To help students develop their answers, you might draw out implications, ask students to clarify words or ideas or to compare their answers, or direct students' attention to parts of the story they may not have considered.

INTRODUCTION TO GREAT BOOKS (HIGH SCHOOL)

Once students in high school understand the process of Shared Inquiry, they can be very self-directed. They should not only be taking notes using the interpretive note source, but they should also be developing their own shorthand for taking notes and jotting down questions that occur to them while reading. During discussion these students should thoroughly explain their answers to an interpretive question. Their answers should be developed fully, drawing on evidence from many parts of the selection. In addition, students should be able to explain how the evidence supports their position. Let them know that you expect them to follow the arguments presented in discussion from person to person and to be civil and respectful when emphasizing a point or trying to get an idea across. When high school students agree or disagree with others, make sure they give their reasons and explain how they read the evidence differently from another participant. High school students should also demonstrate greater facility for incorporating others' ideas into their interpretation of the text.

＊ ＊ ＊

As you begin your Junior Great Books program, remember that you and your students have an exciting and challenging journey ahead. Give yourself time to listen and learn, and enjoy each step along the way.

Chapter Highlight

Ensuring Success in Shared Inquiry Discussion

New leaders come away from the Basic Leader Training Course with a good understanding of the principles of Shared Inquiry Discussion and an eagerness to put them into practice, but they can sometimes make mistakes. The following guidelines will help you avoid some common mistakes many new leaders make.

FOCUS ON INTERPRETATION.

One of the most difficult things to grasp about Shared Inquiry Discussion is that just getting your participants talking, while a good first step, is not enough. In Shared Inquiry Discussion, the ideas must always be focused on the text. Many questions that can generate conversation and even heated debate will not help you reach the goal of increasing students' higher-level reading comprehension. Remember, asking students to speculate about what happens after the story is over or what they would do in a situation similar to one faced by the main character tends to distract them from the story. So does moving too quickly to evaluation— asking students to judge characters or the author before the selection is fully understood. By concentrating on interpretive questions, you will better help participants learn how to read and understand challenging texts.

PROBE IDEAS IN DEPTH.

The informal atmosphere of Shared Inquiry Discussion should not prevent you from asking your students to think critically. One mistake new leaders often make is that of merely polling the group for answers, asking a follow-up question of each student, and not knowing what to do next. Instead, you need to move the group forward by insisting that students provide reasons and evidence for their opinions. Once students understand that you will be probing their ideas in depth, they will meet your high expectations.

AVOID ASKING LEADING QUESTIONS.

Shared Inquiry depends on a special relationship between students and teacher. As a leader of Shared Inquiry, you do not know the best answers to the interpretive questions you ask. You must keep an open mind about what is important in the work in order to maintain an authentic learning situation, one in which you ask questions to learn from your students—not just to test them. Leading participants to a "right" way of looking at the text, in an effort to make sure they get the lesson of a story or absorb your point of view on a nonfiction work, will soon undermine your endeavor to help students think for themselves. For Shared Inquiry Discussion to work, your students must feel that all their ideas and sudden insights—even their mistakes—are valuable steps in the process of building an interpretation. When participants feel confident that even their tentative opinions will be treated with respect, they will be more willing to risk speaking up.

ALLOW ENOUGH TIME FOR PREPARATION.

It cannot be overemphasized that your own direct, patient, and thoughtful encounter with the text—your careful reading, note taking, writing interpretive questions, and reading through the unit in your Teacher's Edition or Leader's Guide—is essential to being a successful leader. If you aren't familiar with the selection and its interpretive issues, you will not be able to ask effective follow-up questions that lead participants to read more closely and involve themselves in the problems of meaning you raise. This is true with regard not only to the writings of the philosophers in Introduction to Great Books but also to the folktales and short stories in the Read-Aloud program and Junior Great Books.

* * *

In Shared Inquiry Discussion, you provide a model of a reader who is curious about a problem and interested in pursuing a solution. Over time, your participants will adopt the habits of mind you display—flexibility, open-mindedness, persistence, and curiosity. Demonstrating these attitudes throughout your Junior Great Books program will have as much impact on your students as any individual discussion you might lead or particular skill you might teach.

Chapter Review

I. As with any learning experience, gaining proficiency in Shared Inquiry—either as a participant or a leader—takes time, practice, and patience.

2. To help students learn the process of Shared Inquiry, model reflective thinking for your students, encourage them when they take time to consider a passage carefully, and ask follow-up questions often to elicit evidence and maintain the focus of discussion.

3. Your first meeting with students will set the tone for your Junior Great Books program. You may find that using one of the mini-units provided in *Getting Started with Junior Great Books* is helpful in introducing students to Shared Inquiry.

4. When introducing students to Shared Inquiry, the most important thing for them to understand is that the process focuses on interpretive questions—questions that have more than one answer that can be supported by the text. Since they will be sharing different opinions and ideas about the story, students must give evidence for their answers.

5. You should expect that your students will come to understand that Shared Inquiry involves expressing curiosity about a text, sharing ideas and opinions, and examining the evidence together. Given time and practice, students will learn that everyone can improve their initial understanding of a text through reflection and sharing of insights.

Appendix

JACK AND THE BEANSTALK

English folktale as told by Joseph Jacobs

There was once upon a time a poor widow who had an only son named Jack and a cow named Milky-white. And all they had to live on was the milk the cow gave every morning, which they carried to the market and sold. But one morning Milky-white gave no milk and they didn't know what to do.

"What shall we do, what shall we do?" said the widow, wringing her hands.

"Cheer up, mother, I'll go and get work somewhere," said Jack.

"We've tried that before, and nobody would take you," said his mother. "We must sell Milky-white and with the money start a shop or something."

"All right, mother," says Jack. "It's market day today, and I'll soon sell Milky-white, and then we'll see what we can do."

So he took the cow's halter in his hand, and off he started. He hadn't gone far when he met a funny-looking old man who said to him: "Good morning, Jack."

"Good morning to you," said Jack, and wondered how he knew his name.

"Well, Jack, and where are you off to?" said the man.

"I'm going to market to sell our cow here."

"Oh, you look the proper sort of chap to sell cows," said the man. "I wonder if you know how many beans make five."

"Two in each hand and one in your mouth," says Jack, as sharp as a needle.

"Right you are," says the man. "And here they are, the very beans themselves," he went on, pulling out of his pocket a number of strange-looking beans. "As you are so sharp," says he, "I don't mind doing a swap with you—your cow for these beans."

"Go along," says Jack. "Wouldn't you like it?"

"Ah! you don't know what these beans are," said the man. "If you plant them overnight, by morning they grow right up to the sky."

"Really?" says Jack. "You don't say so."

"Yes, that is so, and if it doesn't turn out to be true you can have your cow back."

"Right," says Jack, and hands him over Milky-white's halter and pockets the beans.

Back goes Jack home, and as he hadn't gone very far it wasn't dusk by the time he got to his door.

"Back already, Jack?" said his mother. "I see you haven't got Milky-white, so you've sold her. How much did you get for her?"

"You'll never guess, mother," says Jack.

"No, you don't say so. Good boy! Five pounds, ten, fifteen, no, it can't be twenty."

"I told you you couldn't guess. What do you say to these beans; they're magical, plant them overnight and—"

"What!" says Jack's mother. "Have you been such a fool, such a dolt, such an idiot, as to give away my Milky-white, the best milker in the parish, and prime beef to boot, for a set of paltry beans? Take that! Take that! Take that! And as for your precious beans, here they go out of the window. And now off with you to bed. Not a sip shall you drink, and not a bit shall you swallow this very night."

So Jack went upstairs to his little room in the attic, and sad and sorry he was, to be sure, as much for his mother's sake as for the loss of his supper.

At last he dropped off to sleep.

When he woke up, the room looked so funny. The sun was shining into part of it, and yet all the rest was quite dark and shady. So Jack jumped up and dressed himself and went to the window. And what do you think he saw? Why, the beans his mother had thrown out of the window into the garden had sprung up into a big beanstalk which went up and up and up till it reached the sky. So the man spoke truth after all.

The beanstalk grew up quite close past Jack's window, so all he had to do was to open it and give a jump onto the beanstalk, which ran up just like a big ladder. So Jack climbed, and he climbed and he climbed and he climbed and he climbed and he climbed and he climbed till at last he reached the sky. And when he got there he found a long broad road going as straight as a dart. So he walked along and he walked along and he walked along till he came to a great big tall house, and on the doorstep there was a great big tall woman.

"Good morning, mum," says Jack, quite polite-like. "Could you be so kind as to give me some breakfast?" For he hadn't had anything to eat, you know, the night before and was as hungry as a hunter.

"It's breakfast you want, is it?" says the great big tall woman. "It's breakfast you'll be if you don't move off from here. My man is an ogre and there's nothing he likes better than boys broiled on toast. You'd better be moving on or he'll soon be coming."

"Oh! please mum, do give me something to eat, mum. I've had nothing to eat since yesterday morning, really and truly, mum," says Jack. "I may as well be broiled as die of hunger."

Well, the ogre's wife was not half so bad after all. So she took Jack into the kitchen and gave him a chunk of bread and cheese and a jug of milk. But Jack hadn't half finished these when thump! thump! thump! the whole house began to tremble with the noise of someone coming.

"Goodness gracious me! It's my old man," said the ogre's wife. "What on earth shall I do? Come along quick and jump in here." And she bundled Jack into the oven just as the ogre came in.

He was a big one, to be sure. At his belt he had three calves strung up by the heels, and he unhooked them and threw them down on the table and said: "Here, wife, broil me a couple of these for breakfast. Ah! what's this I smell?

Fee-fi-fo-fum,
I smell the blood of an Englishman,
Be he alive, or be he dead
I'll grind his bones to make my bread."

"Nonsense, dear," said his wife, "you're dreaming. Or perhaps you smell the scraps of that little boy you liked so much for yesterday's dinner. Here, you go and have a wash and tidy up, and by the time you come back your breakfast will be ready for you."

So off the ogre went, and Jack was just going to jump out of the oven and run away when the woman told him not. "Wait till he's asleep," says she. "He always has a doze after breakfast."

Well, the ogre had his breakfast, and after that he goes to a big chest and takes out a couple of bags of gold, and down he sits and counts till at last his head began to nod and he began to snore till the whole house shook again.

Then Jack crept out on tiptoe from his oven, and as he was passing the ogre he took one of the bags of gold under his arm, and off he pelters till he came to the beanstalk, and then he threw down the bag of gold, which of course fell into his mother's garden, and then he climbed down and climbed down till at last he got home and told his mother and showed her the gold and said: "Well, mother, wasn't I right about the beans? They are really magical, you see."

So they lived on the bag of gold for some time, but at last they came to the end of it, and Jack made up his mind to try his luck once more up at the top of the beanstalk. So one fine morning he rose up early and got onto the beanstalk, and he climbed and he climbed and he climbed and he climbed and he climbed and he climbed till at last he came out onto the road again and up to the great big tall house he had been to before. There, sure enough, was the great big tall woman standing on the doorstep.

"Good morning, mum," says Jack, as bold as brass. "Could you be so good as to give me something to eat?"

"Go away, my boy," said the big tall woman, "or else my man will eat you up for breakfast. But aren't you the youngster who came here once before? Do you know, that very day, my man missed one of his bags of gold."

"That's strange, mum," says Jack. "I dare say I could tell you something about that, but I'm so hungry I can't speak till I've had something to eat."

Well the big tall woman was so curious that she took him in and gave him something to eat. But he had scarcely begun munching it as slowly as he could when thump! thump! thump! they heard the giant's footstep, and his wife hid Jack away in the oven.

All happened as it did before. In came the ogre as he did before, said "Fee-fi-fo-fum," and had his breakfast of three broiled oxen. Then he said: "Wife, bring me the hen that lays the golden eggs." So she brought it, and the ogre said "Lay," and it laid an egg all of gold. And then the ogre began to nod his head and to snore till the house shook.

Then Jack crept out of the oven on tiptoe and caught hold of the golden hen, and was off before you could say "Jack Robinson." But this time the hen gave a cackle which woke the ogre, and just as Jack got out of the house he heard him calling: "Wife, wife, what have you done with my golden hen?"

And the wife said: "Why, my dear?"

But that was all Jack heard, for he rushed off to the beanstalk and climbed down like a house on fire. And when he got home he showed his mother the wonderful hen and said "Lay," to it; and it laid a golden egg every time he said "Lay."

Well, Jack was not content, and it wasn't very long before he determined to have another try at his luck up there at the top of the beanstalk. So one fine morning he rose up early, and got onto the beanstalk, and he climbed and he climbed and he climbed and he climbed till he got to the top. But this time he knew better than to go straight to the ogre's house. And when he got near it he waited behind a bush till he saw the ogre's wife come out with a pail to get some water, and then he crept into the house and got into the copper. He hadn't been there long when he heard thump! thump! thump! as before, and in come the ogre and his wife.

"Fee-fi-fo-fum, I smell the blood of an Englishman," cried out the ogre. "I smell him, wife, I smell him."

"Do you, my dearie?" says the ogre's wife. "Then if it's that little rogue that stole your gold and the hen that laid the golden eggs, he's sure to have got into the oven." And they both rushed to the oven. But Jack wasn't there, luckily, and the ogre's wife said: "There you are again with your fee-fi-fo-fum. Why of course it's the boy you caught last night that I've just broiled for your breakfast. How forgetful I am, and how care-less you are not to know the difference between live and dead after all these years."

So the ogre sat down to the breakfast and ate it, but every now and then he would mutter: "Well, I could have sworn—" and he'd get up and search the larder and the cupboards, and everything, only luckily he didn't think of the copper.

After breakfast was over, the ogre called out: "Wife, wife, bring me my golden harp." So she brought it and put it on the table before him. Then he said "Sing!" and the golden harp sang most beautifully. And it went on singing till the ogre fell asleep and commenced to snore like thunder.

Then Jack lifted up the copper lid very quietly and got down like a mouse and crept on hands and knees till he came to the table, when up he crawled, caught hold of the golden harp, and dashed with it towards the door. But the harp called out quite loud "Master! Master!" and the ogre woke up just in time to see Jack running off with his harp.

Jack ran as fast as he could, and the ogre came rushing after, and would soon have caught him only Jack had a start and dodged him a bit and knew where he was going. When he got to the beanstalk the ogre was not more than twenty yards away, when suddenly he saw Jack disappear, and when he came to the end of the road he saw Jack underneath climbing down for dear life. Well, the ogre didn't like trusting himself to such a ladder, and he stood and waited, so Jack got another start. But just then the harp cried out "Master! Master!" and the ogre swung himself down onto the beanstalk, which shook with his weight.

Down climbs Jack, and after him climbed the ogre. By this time Jack had climbed down and climbed down and climbed down till he was very nearly home. So he called out: "Mother! Mother! Bring me an axe, bring me an axe." And his mother came rushing out with the axe in her hand, but when she came to the beanstalk she stood stock still with fright for there she saw the ogre with his legs just through the clouds.

But Jack jumped down and got hold of the axe and gave a chop at the beanstalk which cut it half in two. The ogre felt the beanstalk shake and quiver so he stopped to see what was the matter. Then Jack gave another chop with the axe, and the beanstalk was cut in two and began to topple over. Then the ogre fell down and broke his crown, and the beanstalk came toppling after.

Then Jack showed his mother his golden harp, and what with showing that and selling the golden eggs, Jack and his mother became very rich, and he married a great princess, and they lived happy ever after.

A GAME OF CATCH

Richard Wilbur

Monk and Glennie were playing catch on the side lawn of the firehouse when Scho caught sight of them. They were good at it, for seventh graders, as anyone could see right away. Monk, wearing a catcher's mitt, would lean easily sidewise and back, with one leg lifted and his throwing hand almost down to the grass, and then lob the white ball straight up into the sunlight. Glennie would shield his eyes with his left hand and, just as the ball fell past him, snag it with a little dart of his glove. Then he would burn the ball straight toward Monk, and it would spank into the round mitt and sit, like a still-life apple on a plate, until Monk flipped it over into his right hand and, with a negligent flick of his hanging arm, gave Glennie a fast grounder.

They were going on and on like that, in a kind of slow, mannered, luxurious dance in the sun, their faces perfectly blank and entranced, when Glennie noticed Scho dawdling along the other side of the street and called hello to him. Scho crossed over and stood at the front edge of the lawn, near an apple tree, watching.

"Got your glove?" asked Glennie after a time. Scho obviously hadn't.

"You could give me some easy grounders," said Scho. "But don't burn 'em."

"All right," Glennie said. He moved off a little, so the three of them formed a triangle, and they passed the ball around for about five minutes, Monk tossing easy grounders to Scho, Scho throwing to Glennie, and Glennie burning them in to Monk. After a while, Monk began to throw them back to

Glennie once or twice before he let Scho have his grounder, and finally Monk gave Scho a fast, bumpy grounder that hopped over his shoulder and went into the brake on the other side of the street.

"Not so hard," called Scho as he ran across to get it.

"You should've had it," Monk shouted.

It took Scho a little while to find the ball among the ferns and dead leaves, and when he saw it, he grabbed it up and threw it toward Glennie. It struck the trunk of the apple tree, bounced back at an angle, and rolled steadily and stupidly onto the cement apron in front of the firehouse, where one of the trucks was parked. Scho ran hard and stopped it just before it rolled under the truck, and this time he carried it back to his former position on the lawn and threw it carefully to Glennie.

"I got an idea," said Glennie. "Why don't Monk and I catch for five minutes more, and then you can borrow one of our gloves?"

"That's all right with me," said Monk. He socked his fist into his mitt, and Glennie burned one in.

"All right," Scho said, and went over and sat under the tree. There in the shade he watched them resume their skillful play. They threw lazily fast or lazily slow—high, low, or wide—and always handsomely, their expressions serene, changeless, and forgetful. When Monk missed a low backhand catch, he walked indolently after the ball and, hardly even looking, flung it sidearm for an imaginary put-out. After a good while of this, Scho said, "Isn't it five minutes yet?"

"One minute to go," said Monk, with a fraction of a grin.

Scho stood up and watched the ball slap back and forth for several minutes more, and then he turned and pulled himself up into the crotch of the tree.

"Where are you going?" Monk asked.

"Just up the tree," Scho said.

"I guess he doesn't want to catch," said Monk.

Scho went up and up through the fat light-gray branches until they grew slender and bright and gave under him. He found a place where several supple branches were knit to make a dangerous chair, and sat there with his head coming out of the leaves into the sunlight. He could see the two other boys down below, the ball going back and forth between them as if they were bowling on the grass, and Glennie's crew-cut head looking like a sea urchin.

"I found a wonderful seat up here," Scho said loudly. "If I don't fall out." Monk and Glennie didn't look up or comment and so he began jouncing gently in his chair of branches and singing "Yo-ho, heave ho" in an exaggerated way.

"Do you know what, Monk?" he announced in a few moments. "I can make you two guys do anything I want. Catch that ball, Monk! Now you catch it, Glennie!"

"I was going to catch it anyway," Monk suddenly said. "You're not making anybody do anything when they're already going to do it anyway."

"I made you say what you just said," Scho replied joyfully.

"No, you didn't," said Monk, still throwing and catching but now less serenely absorbed in the game.

"That's what I wanted you to say," Scho said.

The ball bounded off the rim of Monk's mitt and plowed into a gladiolus bed beside the firehouse, and Monk ran to get it while Scho jounced in his treetop and sang, "I wanted you to miss that. Anything you do is what I wanted you to do."

"Let's quit for a minute," Glennie suggested.

"We might as well, until the peanut gallery shuts up," Monk said.

They went over and sat crosslegged in the shade of the tree. Scho looked down between his legs and saw them on the dim, spotty ground, saying nothing to one another. Glennie soon began abstractedly spinning his glove between his palms; Monk pulled his nose and stared out across the lawn.

"I want you to mess around with your nose, Monk," said Scho, giggling. Monk withdrew his hand from his face.

"Do that with your glove, Glennie," Scho persisted. "Monk, I want you to pull up hunks of grass and chew on it."

Glennie looked up and saw a self-delighted, intense face staring down at him through the leaves. "Stop being a dope and come down and we'll catch for a few minutes," he said.

Scho hesitated, and then said, in a tentatively mocking voice, "That's what I wanted you to say."

"All right, then, nuts to you," said Glennie.

"Why don't you keep quiet and stop bothering people?" Monk asked.

"I made you say that," Scho replied, softly.

"Shut up," Monk said.

"I made you say that, and I want you to be standing there looking sore. And I want you to climb up the tree. I'm making you do it!"

Monk was scrambling up through the branches, awkward in his haste, and getting snagged on twigs. His face was furious and foolish, and he kept telling Scho to shut up, shut up, shut up, while the other's exuberant and panicky voice poured down upon his head.

"Now you shut up or you'll be sorry," Monk said, breathing hard as he reached up and threatened to shake the cradle of slight branches in which Scho was sitting.

"I *want*—" Scho screamed as he fell. Two lower branches broke his rustling, crackling fall, but he landed on his back with a deep thud and lay still, with a strangled look on his face and his eyes clenched. Glennie knelt down and asked breathlessly, "Are you OK, Scho? Are you OK?" while Monk swung down through the leaves crying that honestly he hadn't even touched him, the crazy guy just let go. Scho doubled up and turned over on his right side, and now both the other boys knelt beside him, pawing at his shoulder and begging to know how he was.

Then Scho rolled away from them and sat partly up, still struggling to get his wind but forcing a species of smile onto his face.

"I'm sorry, Scho," Monk said. "I didn't mean to make you fall."

Scho's voice came out weak and gravelly, in gasps. "I meant—you to do it. You—had to. You can't do—anything—unless I want—you to."

Glennie and Monk looked helplessly at him as he sat there, breathing a bit more easily and smiling fixedly, with tears in his eyes. Then they picked up their gloves and the ball, walked over to the street, and went slowly away down the sidewalk, Monk punching his fist into the mitt, Glennie juggling the ball between glove and hand.

From under the apple tree, Scho, still bent over a little for lack of breath, croaked after them in triumph and misery, "I want you to do whatever you're going to do for the whole rest of your life!" 🦐

Index